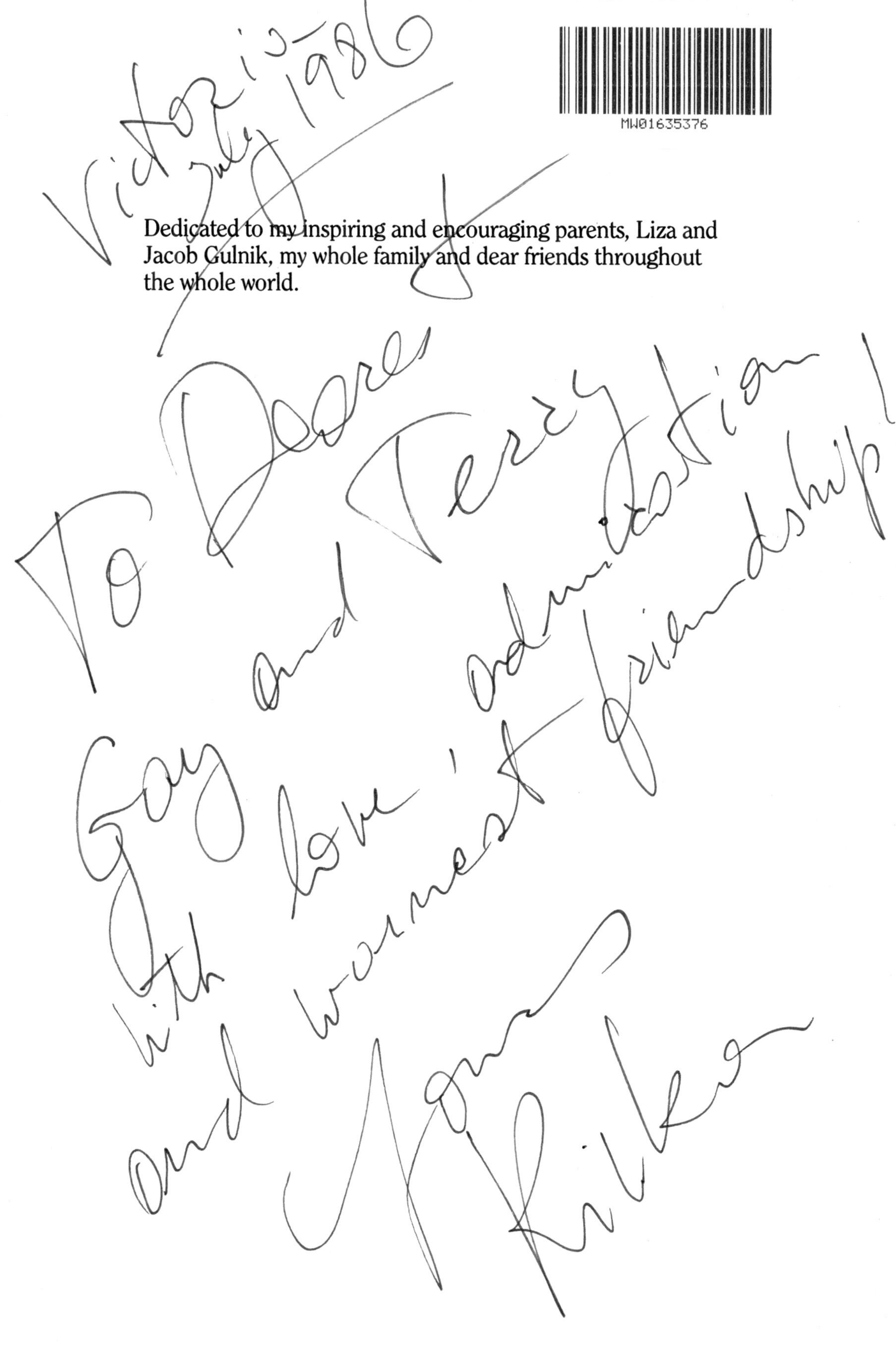

Dedicated to my inspiring and encouraging parents, Liza and Jacob Gulnik, my whole family and dear friends throughout the whole world.

BIRDS OF ANOTHER FEATHER . . .
MY MUSICAL COLLEAGUES

BIRDS OF ANOTHER FEATHER . . . MY MUSICAL COLLEAGUES

Drawings by

RIVKA GOLANI

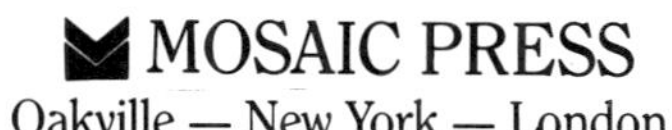

MOSAIC PRESS
Oakville — New York — London

CANADIAN CATALOGUING IN PUBLICATION DATA

Golani-Erdész, Rivka, 1946-
Birds of another feather-- my musical colleagues

ISBN 0-88962-308-2 (bound). - ISBN 0-88962-309-0 (pbk.)

1. Musicians - Caricatures and cartoons.
2. Musicians - Canada - Caricatures and cartoons.
I. Title.

ML87.G64 1985 780'.92'2 C85-099873-5

Published by Mosaic Press, P.O. Box 1032, Oakville, Ontario, L6J 5E9, Canada. Offices and warehouse at 1252 Speers Road, Unit 10, Oakville, Ontario, L6L 5N9, Canada.

Published with the assistance of the Canada Council and the Ontario Arts Council.

Typeset by Lount Graphics Ltd.
Printed and bound in Canada.
Designed by Rita Vogel.
ISBN 0-88962-308-2 cloth
0-88962-309-0 paper

MOSAIC PRESS:

In the United States: Flatiron Book Distributors, 1170 Broadway, Suite 807, New York, N.Y., 10001, USA.

In the U.K.: John Calder (Publishers) Ltd., 18 Brewer Street, London, W1R 4AS, England.

In Australia: Bookwise International, Jeanes Street, Beverley, South Australia, 5007, Australia.

THE ART OF RIVKA GOLANI

RIVKA GOLANI, universally acclaimed as the most celebrated viola virtuoso of our time, has also emerged on the international art scene as an extraordinary artist-painter.

There is, undoubtedly, a natural link between Rivka's phenomenal interpretation of music — ranging from the classics and romantics to the very modern composers — and the unique ability of self-expression found in her art works.

"It is a need I have . . ." Rivka often says; the need to express her inner world, the hardships and joys of her life, her moods and inspirations in the art of painting and drawing.

From the monumental abstract canvases, painted with her pallete in bold, vivid colours to the subtle, refined shapes of the charming, humorous drawings, her art reflects her unusual ability to overcome those laws of gravity, that hold others down . . .

While this remarkably versatile artist conveys to us on her magical viola the mastery of the art of music, she also shares with us her wit and genial sense of humour, shaping forms of ideas that grow in her imagination in her paintings and drawings . . .

Instinctively, transforming her environment of human characters, she draws through the prism of her alegorical images a galaxy of funny, lovable creatures . . .

Consequently, a genial creative stroke produced this very unique collection of marvelous drawings by a genuine Master.

Igor I. Kuchinsky PhD.

INTRODUCTION

Every so often, unable to come to terms with my associates — colleagues — I have found myself thrown into a world protected by my own imagination . . . .

And here, in the most humorous way, I present visual expressions of those I worked with, including conductors, composers, players throughout the world.

I do believe that the greatest artists — the true creators — are gifted with fantastic imagination and humour.

As some of my colleagues are 'up there' just to please the crowd, unable to appreciate a joke . . . I could not identify my creatures.

And now it is up to their wild imagination to travel through this book and to identify themselves!

With the very best intentions and lots of love,

Rivka

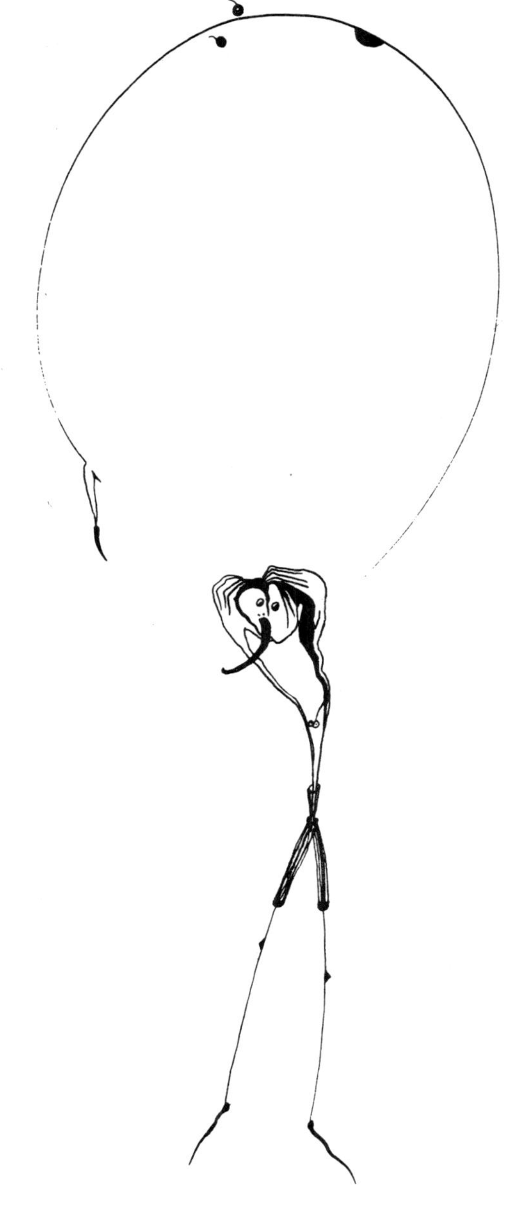

Self portrait ...

SOLOISTS

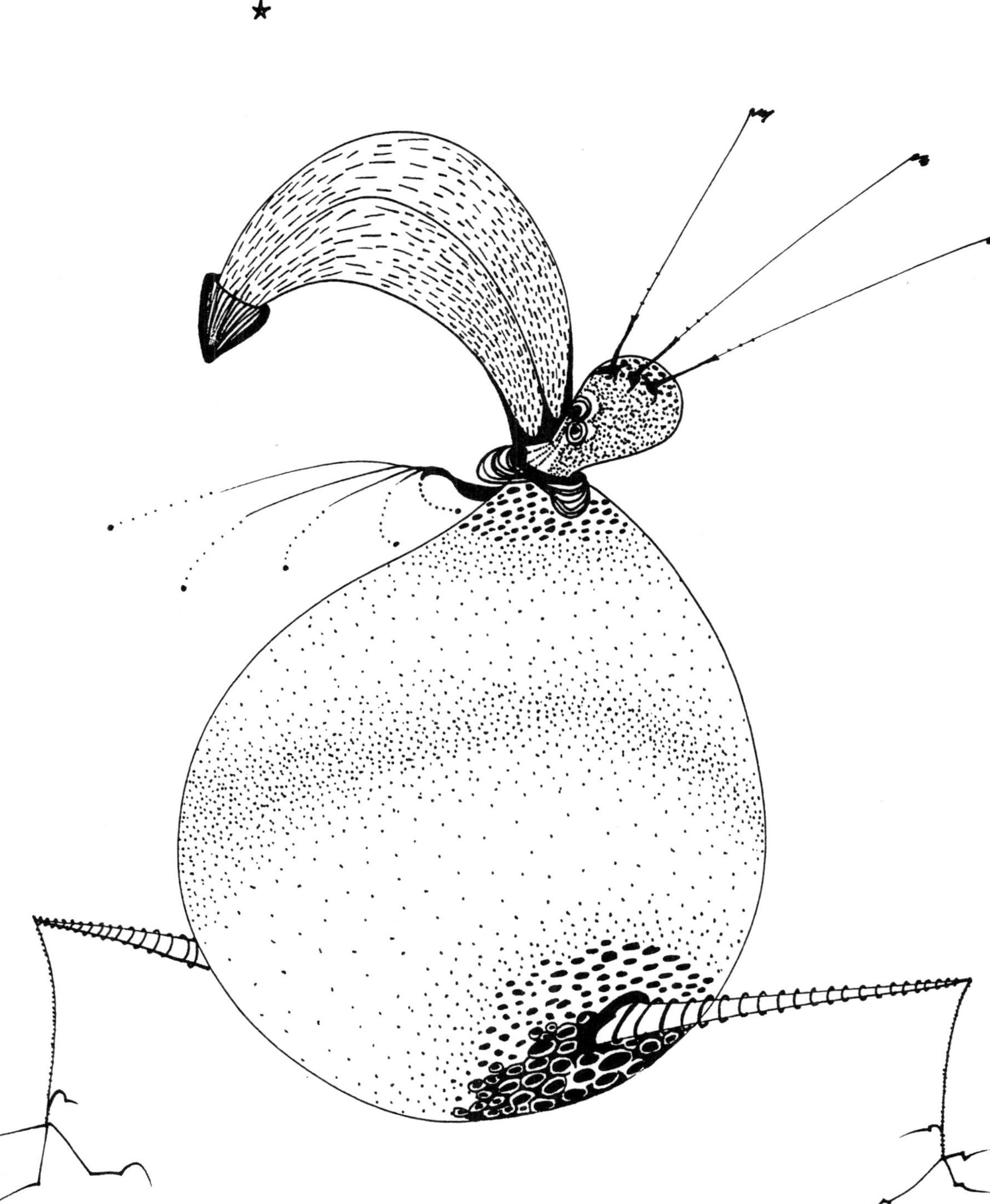

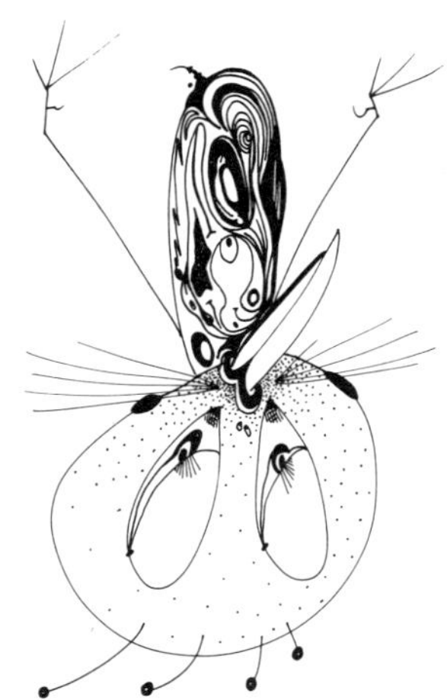

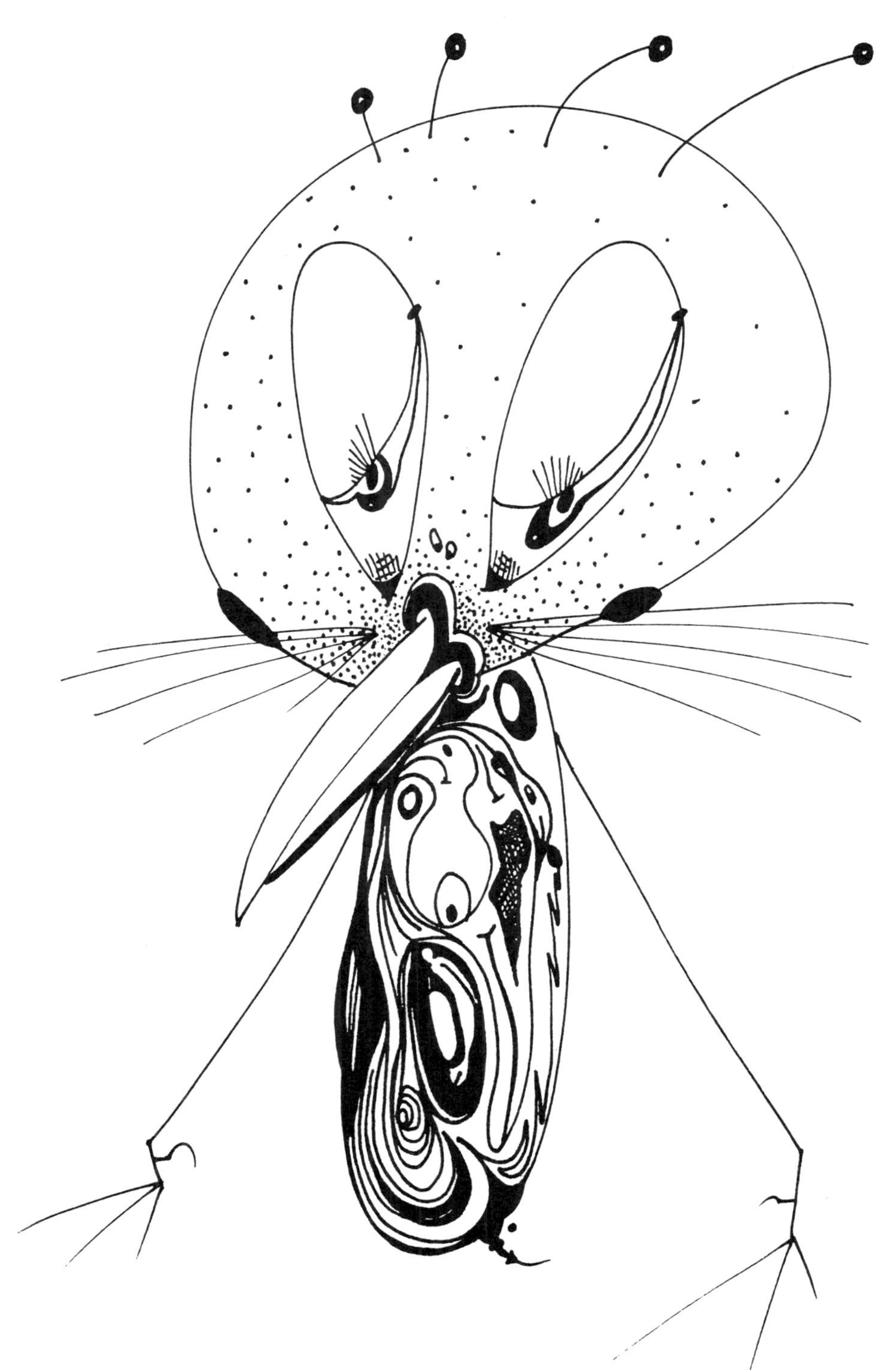

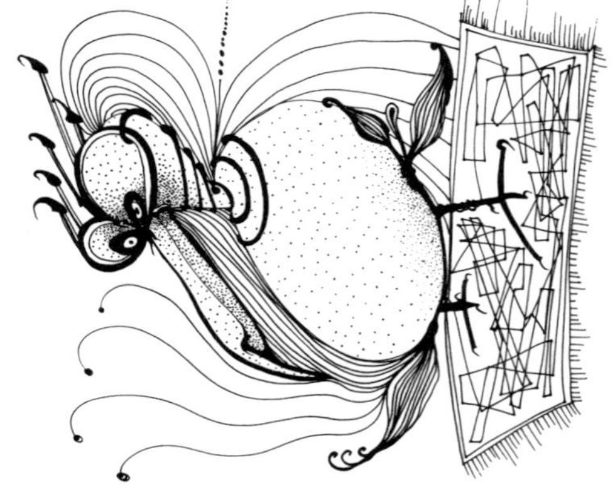

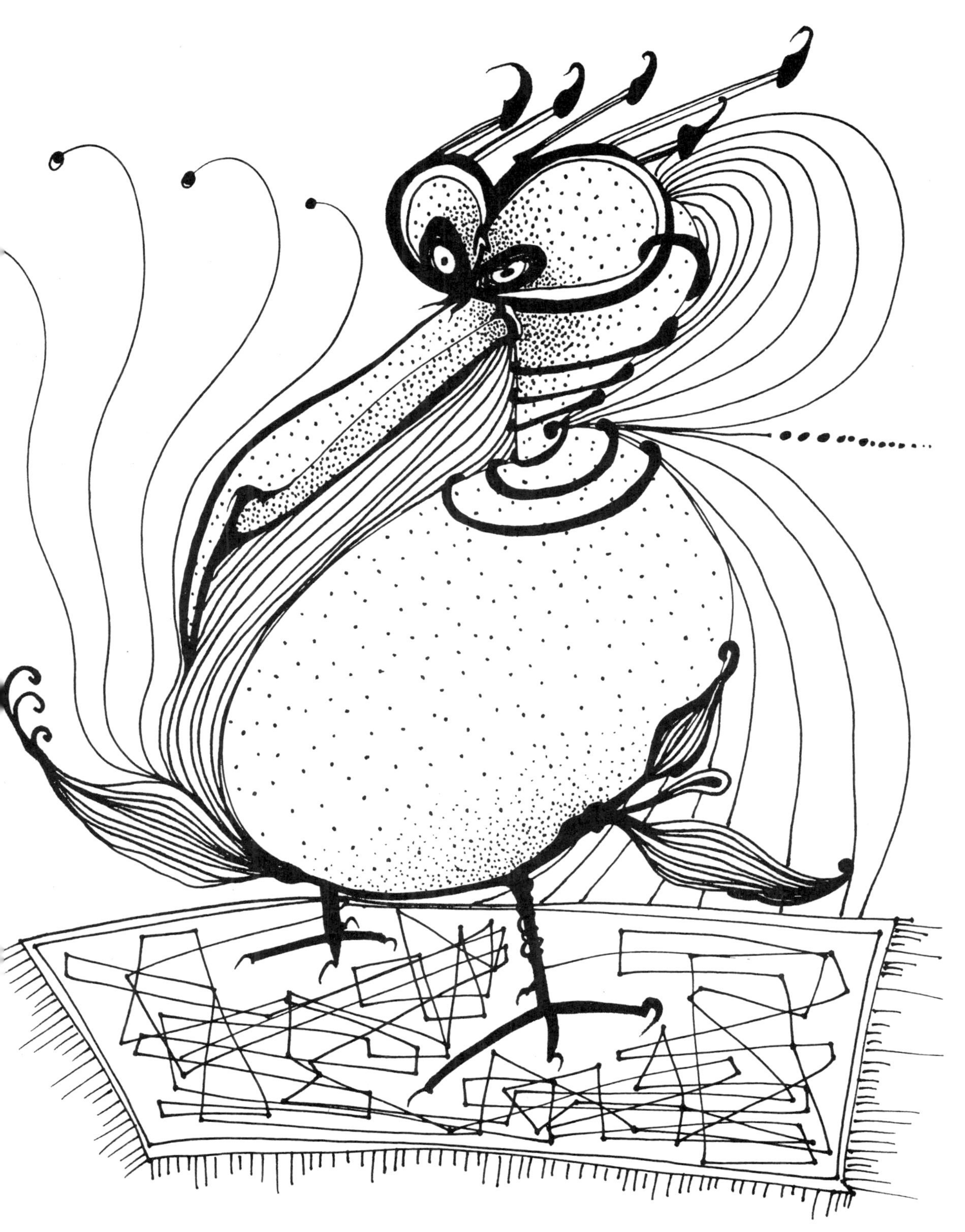

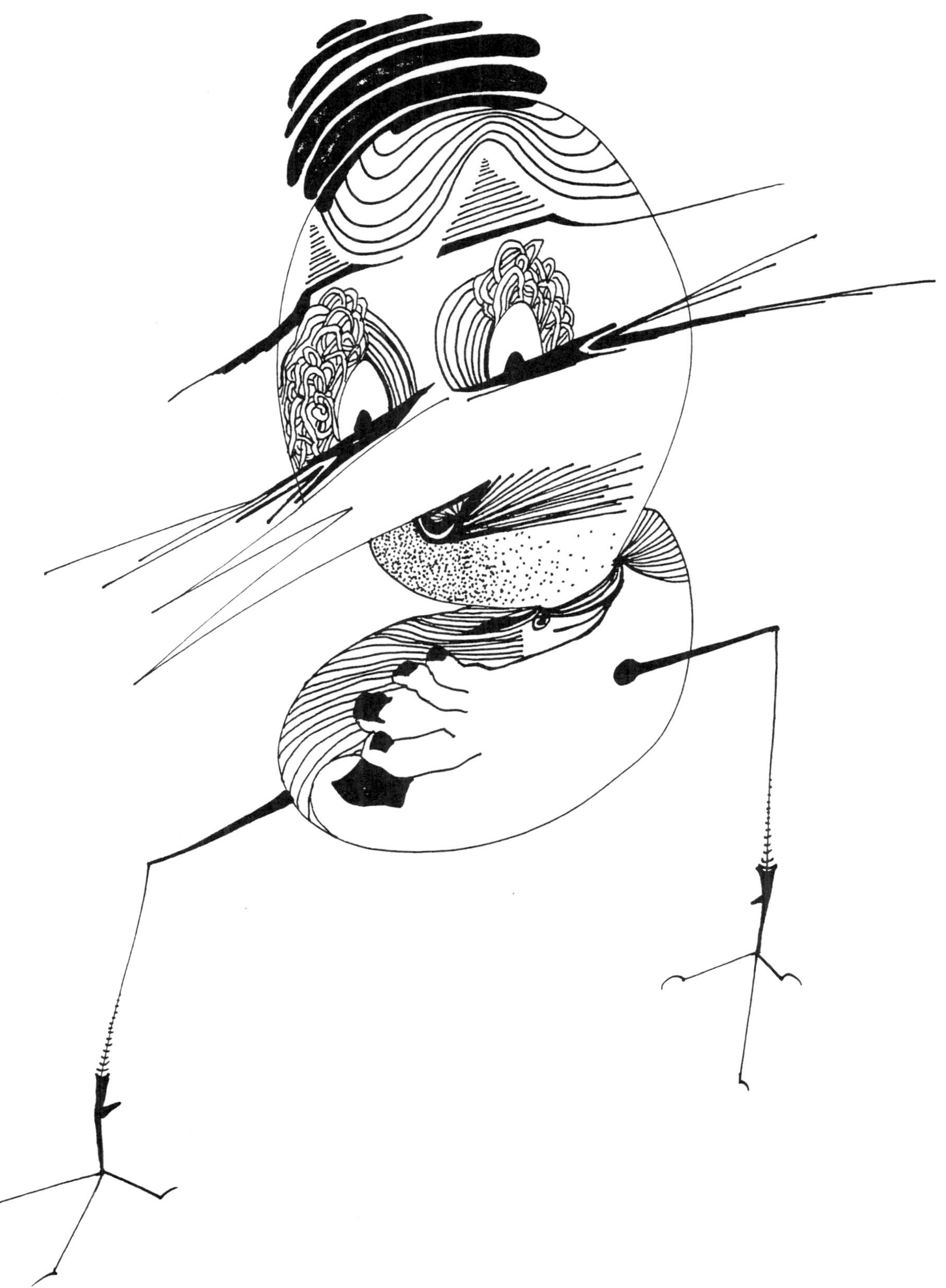

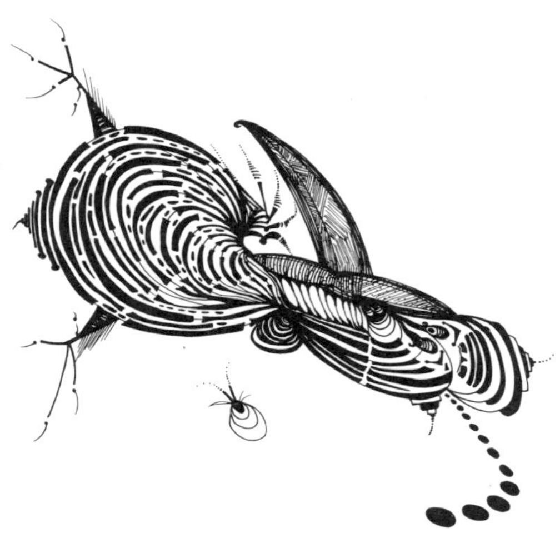

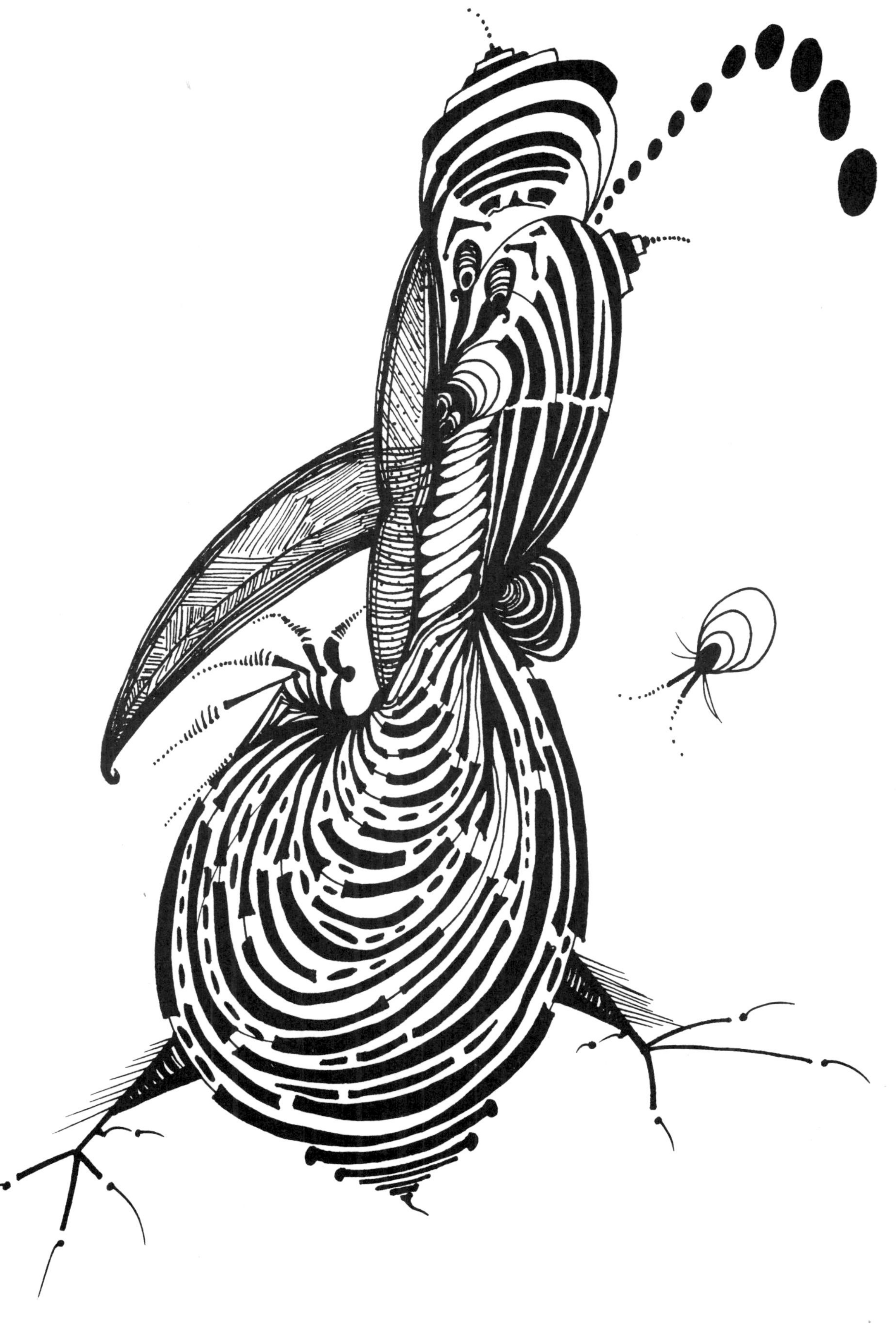

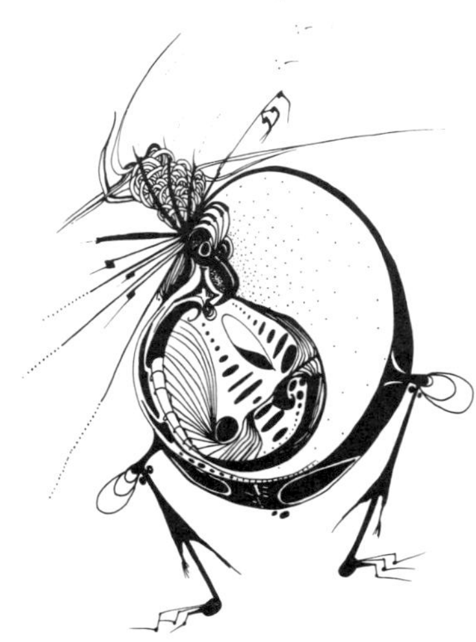

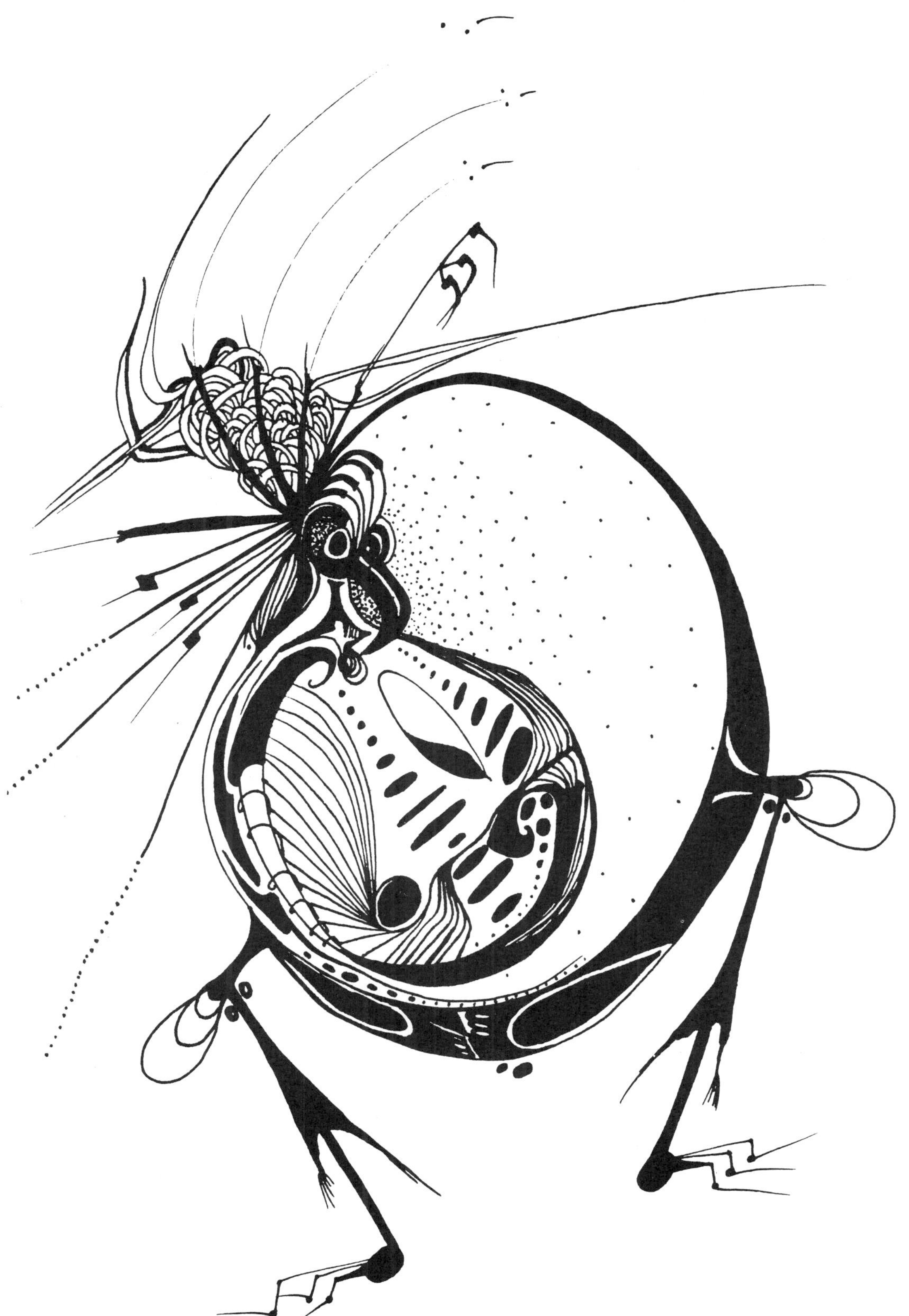

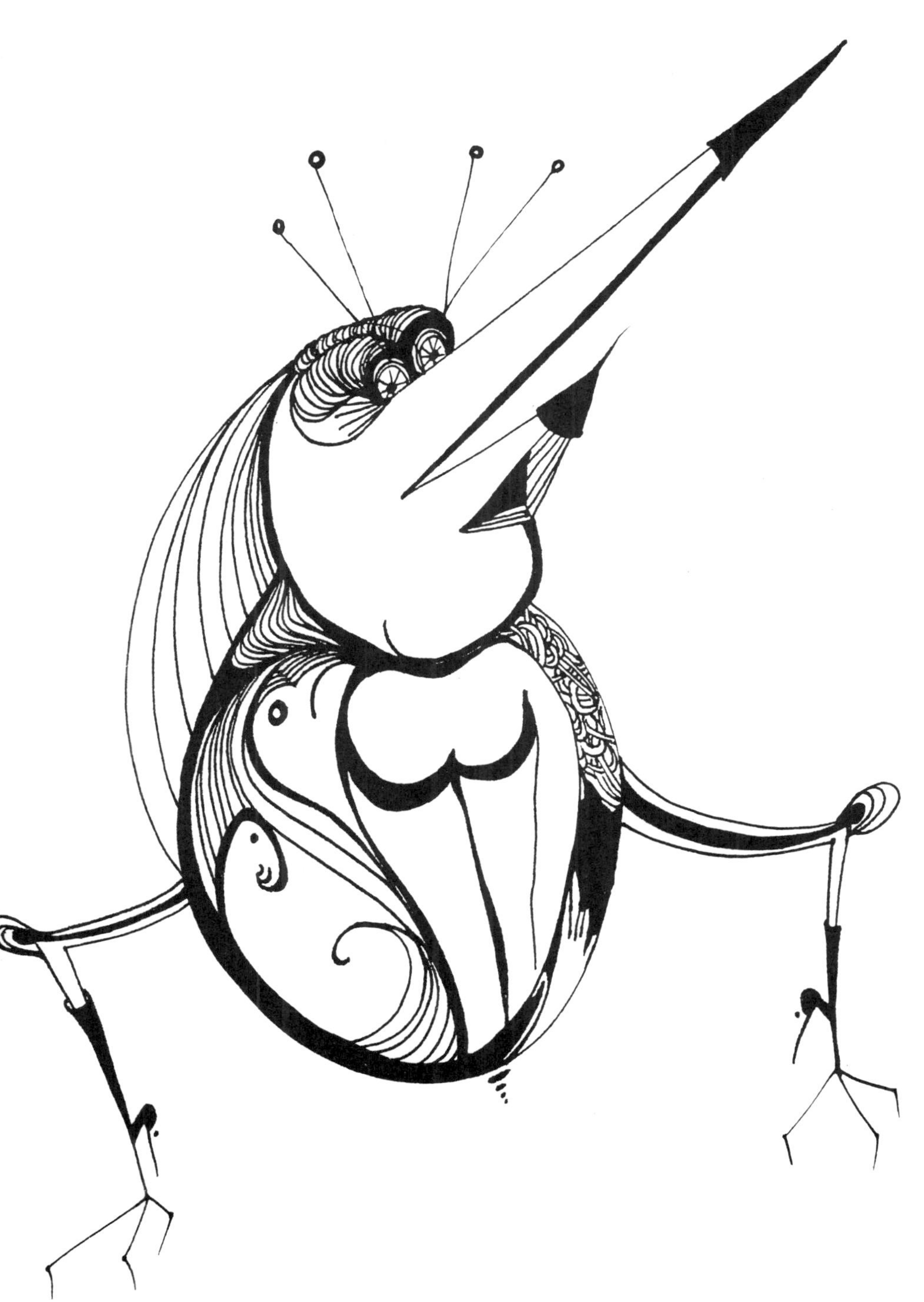

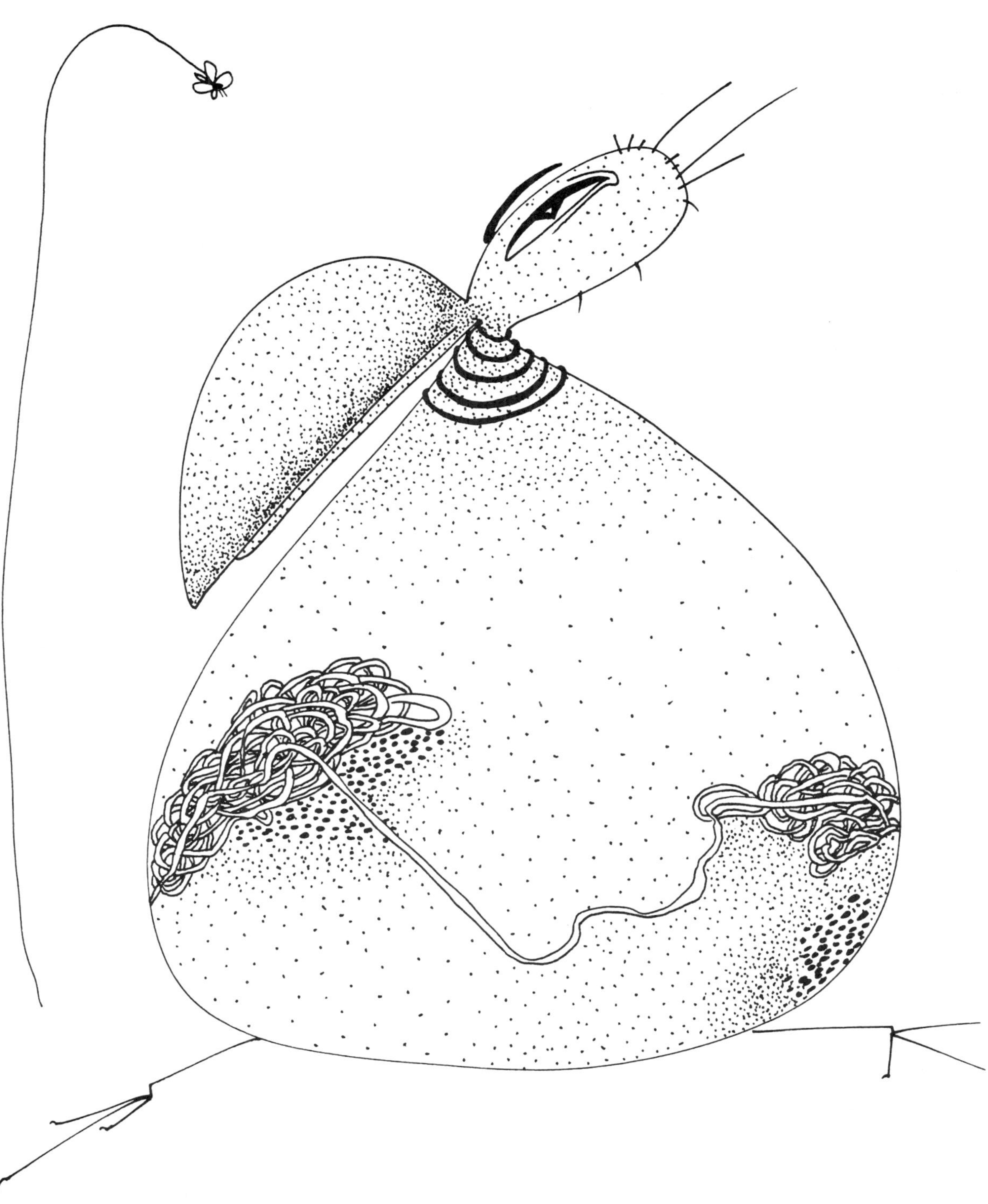

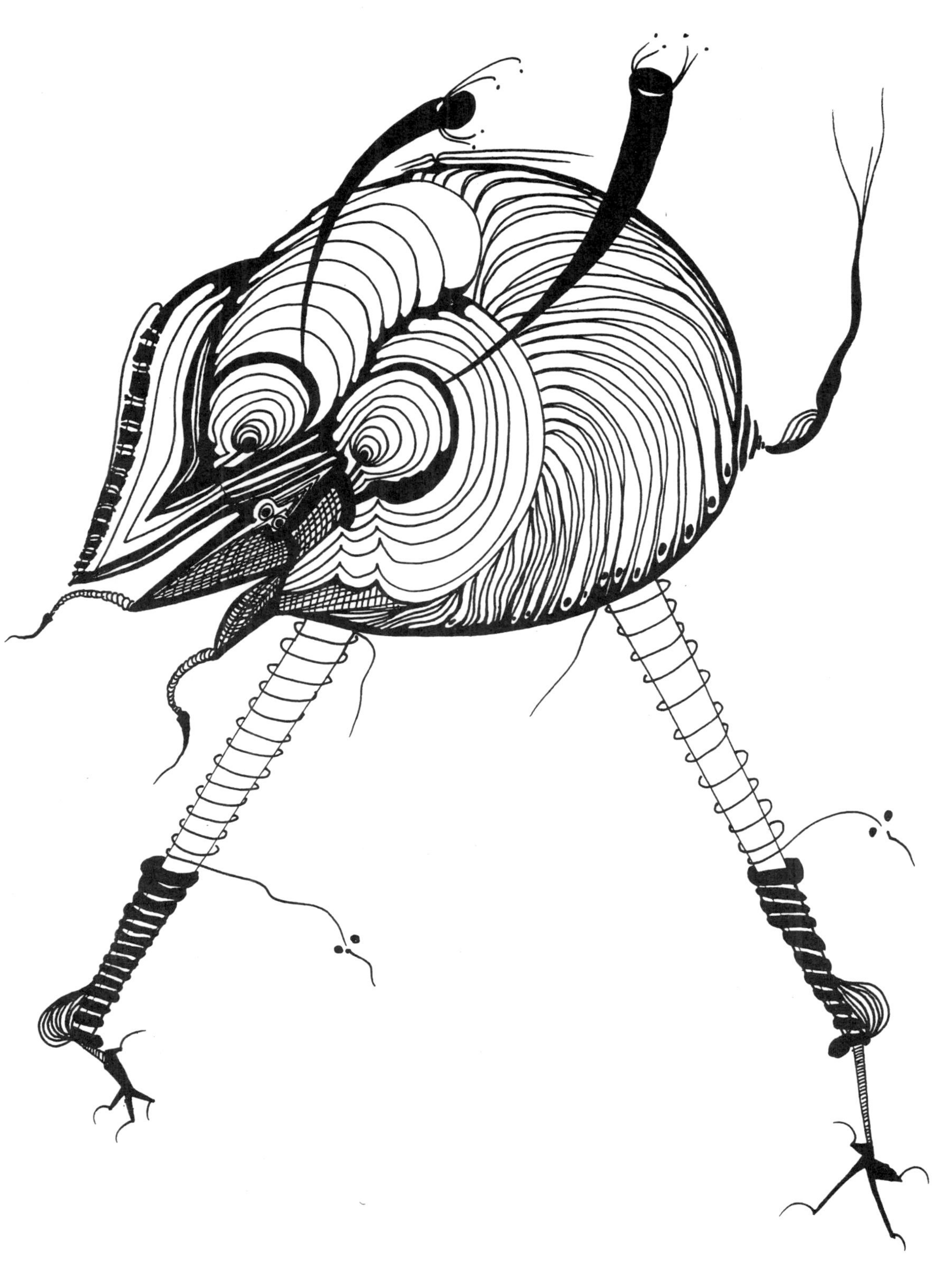

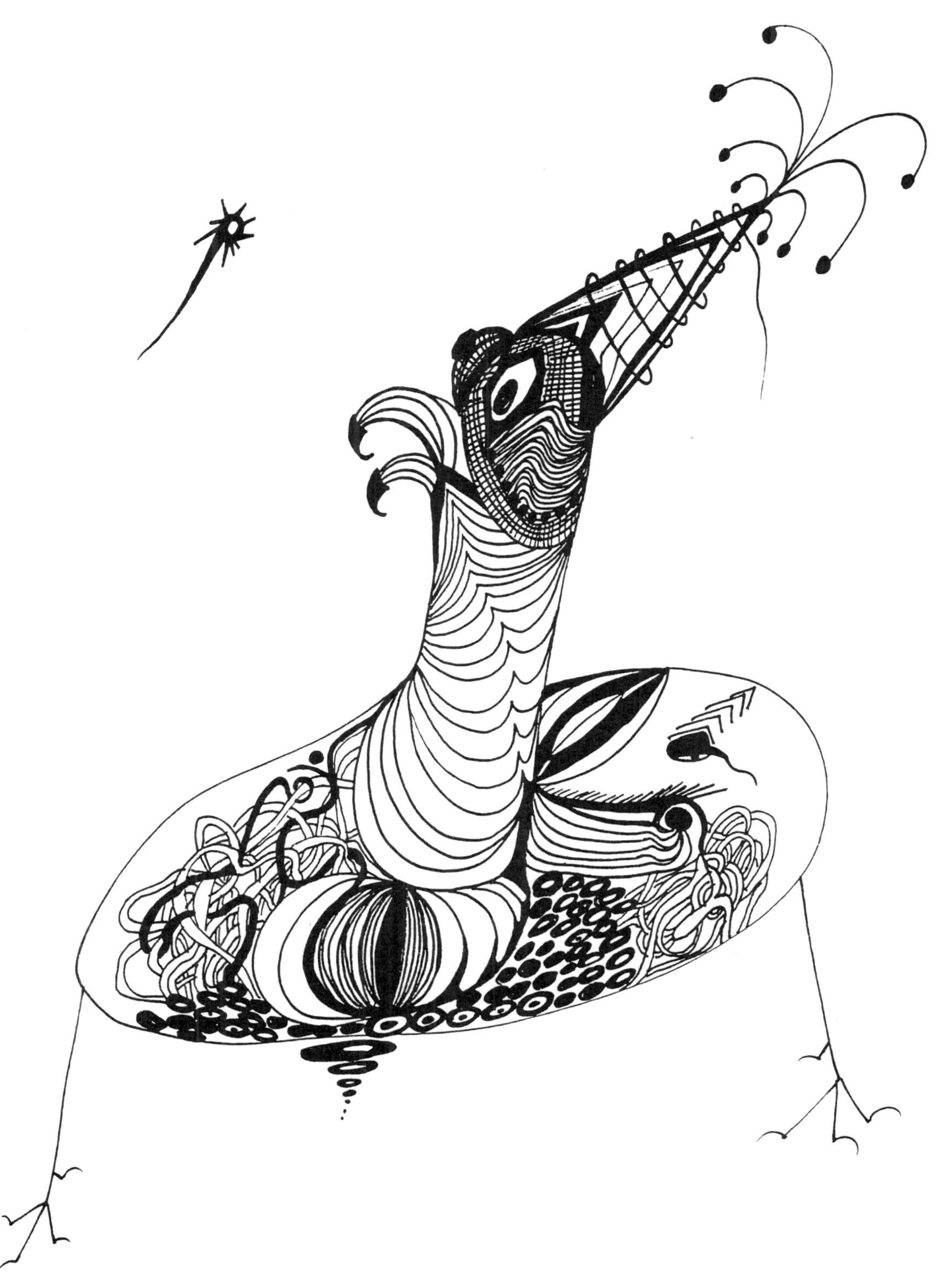

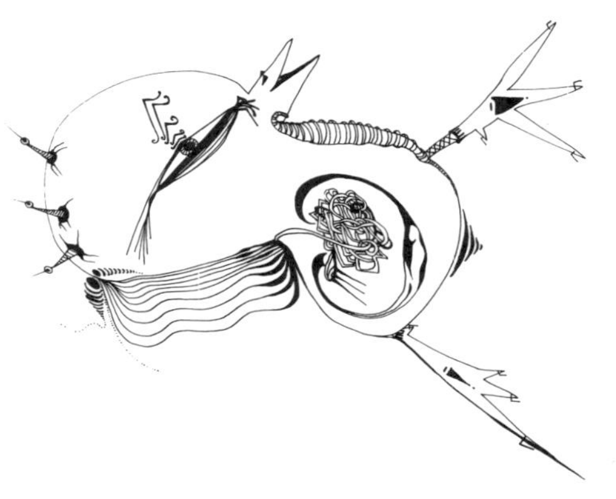

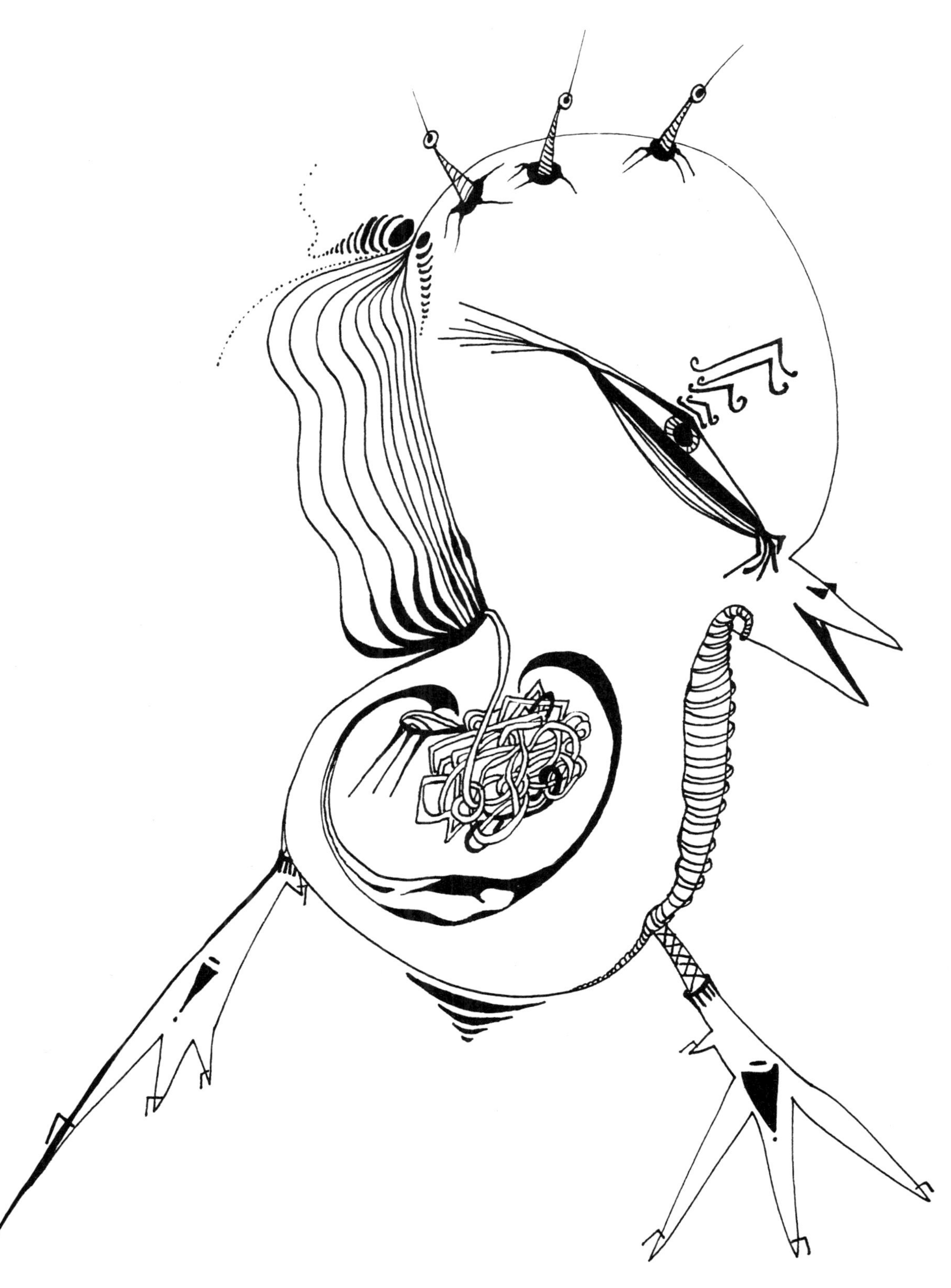

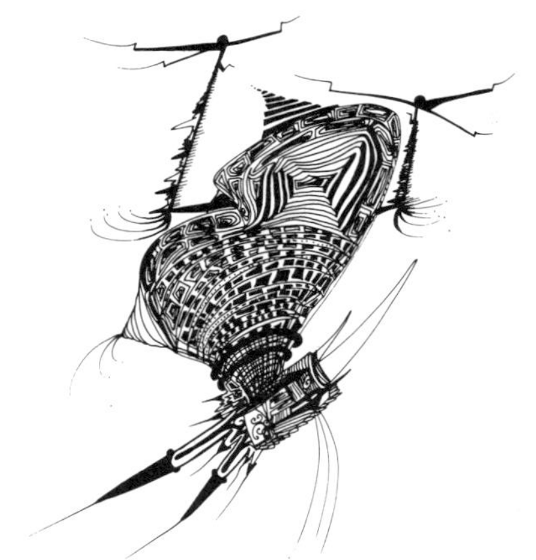

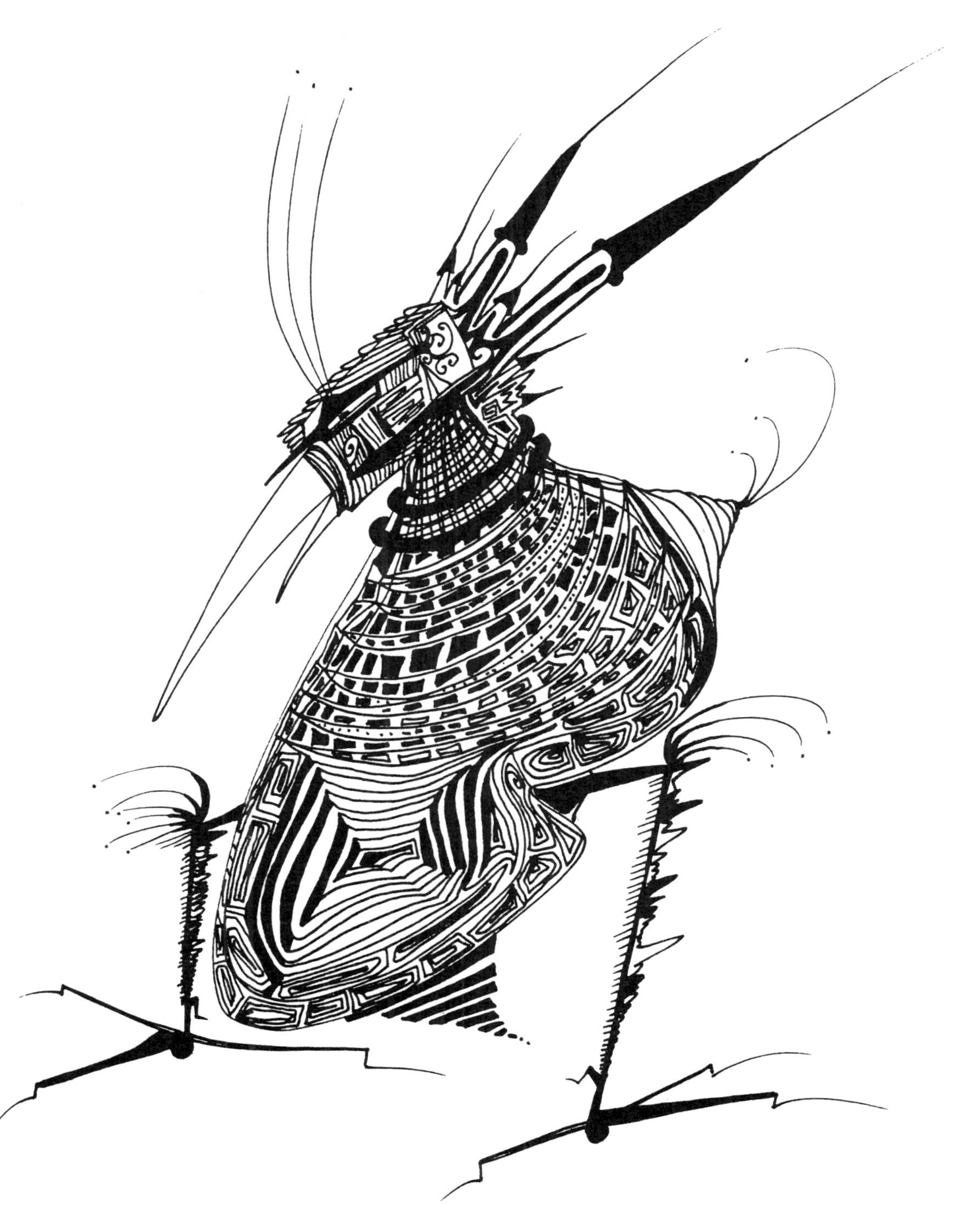

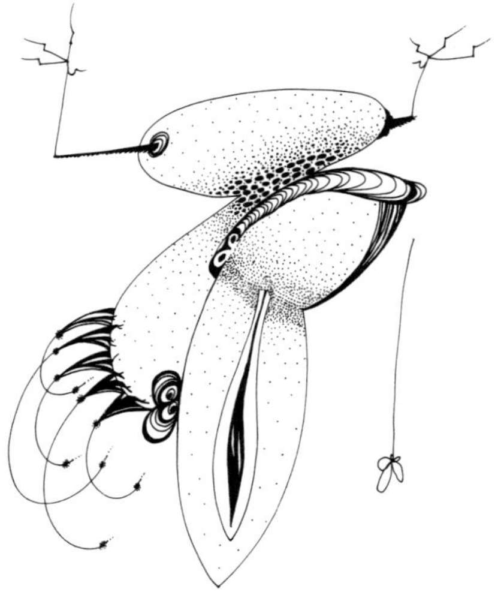

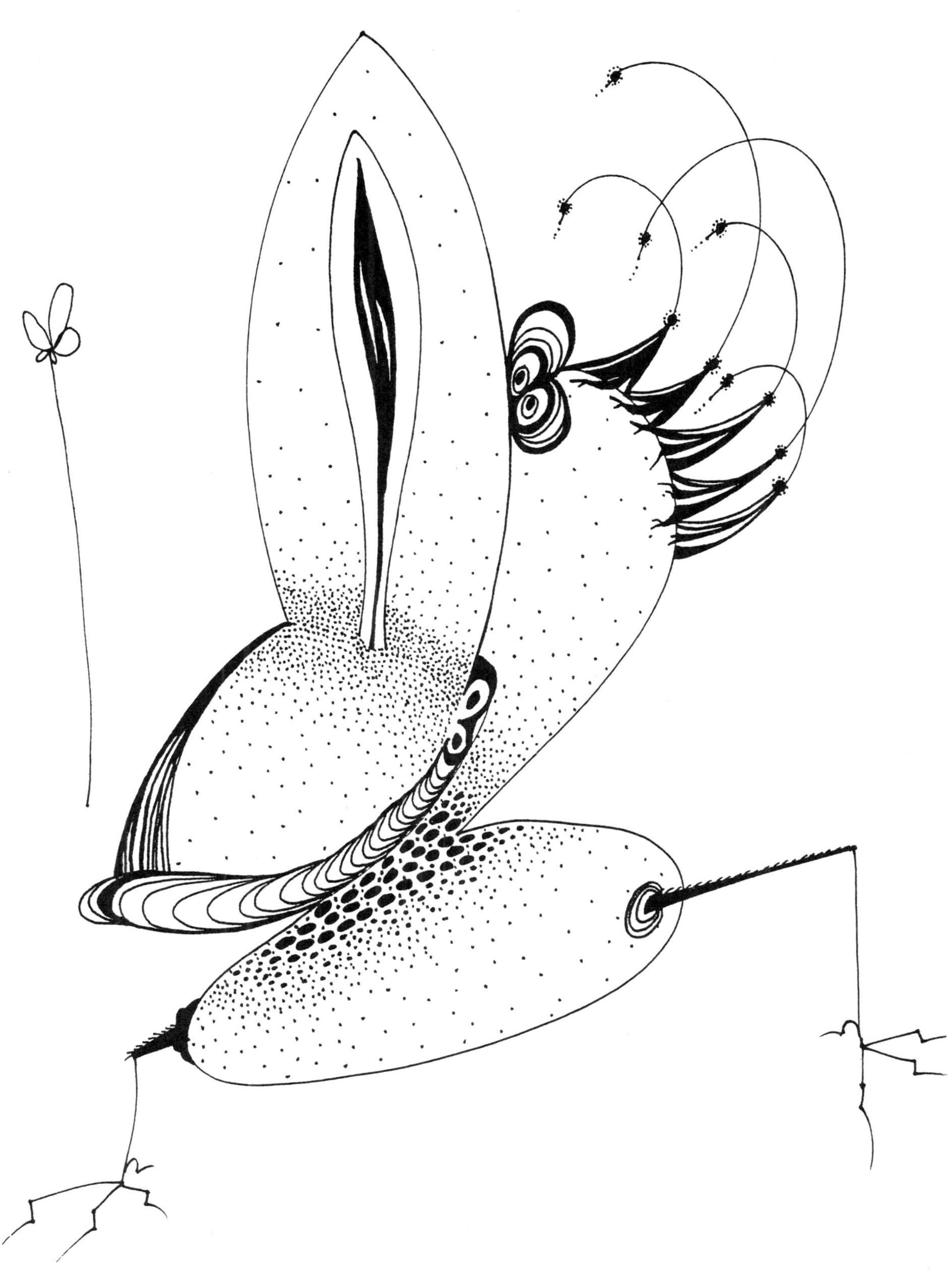

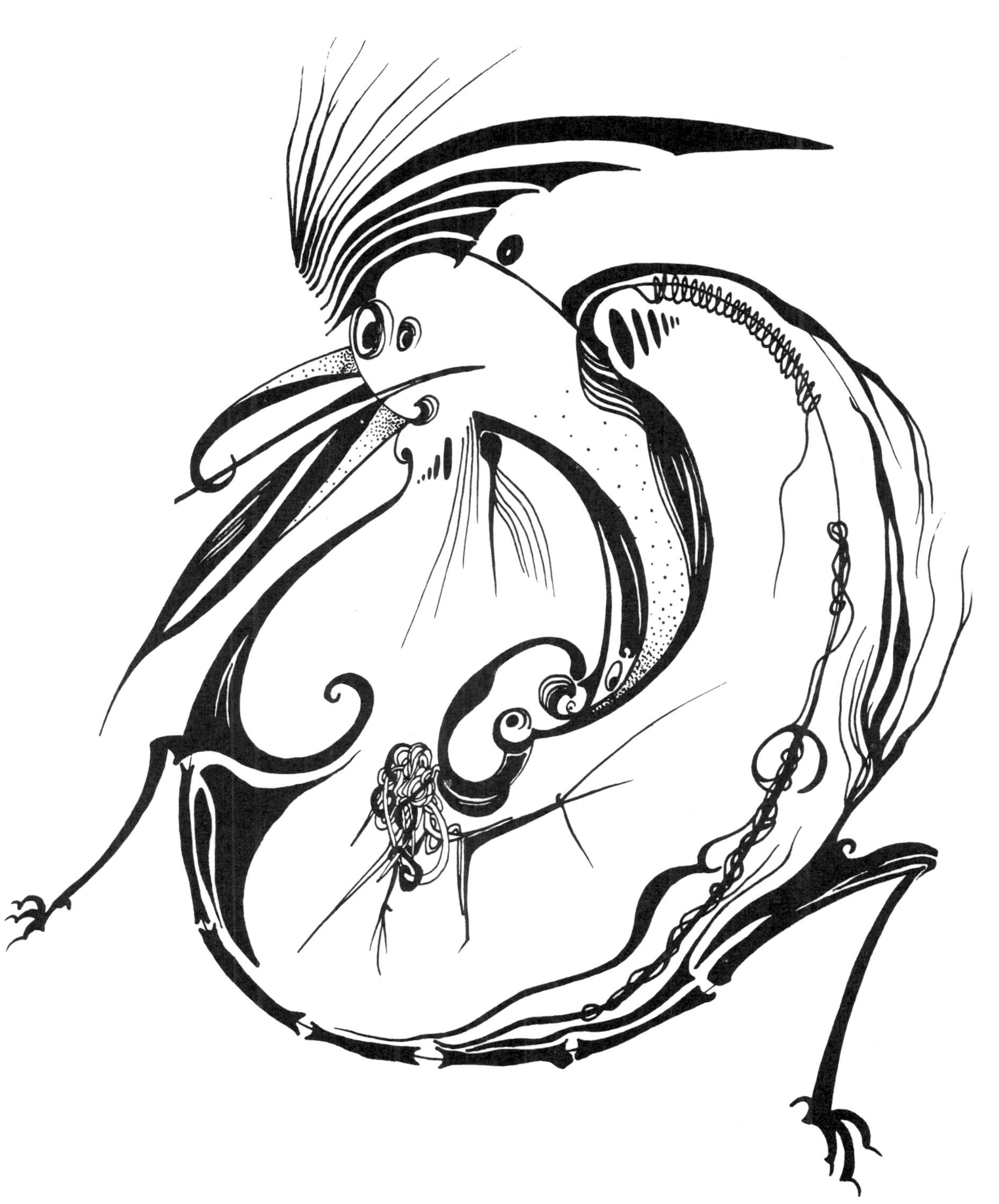

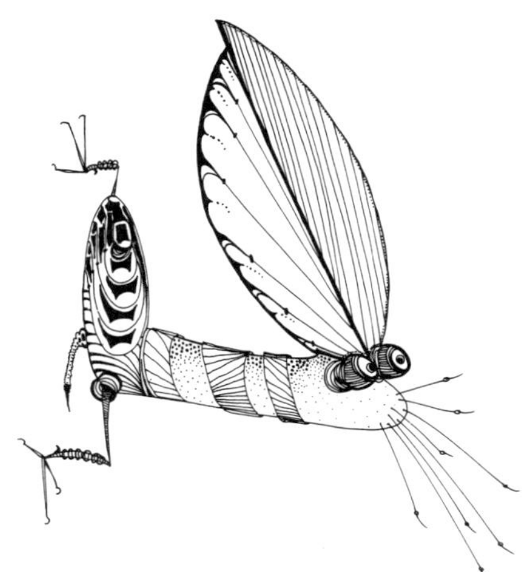

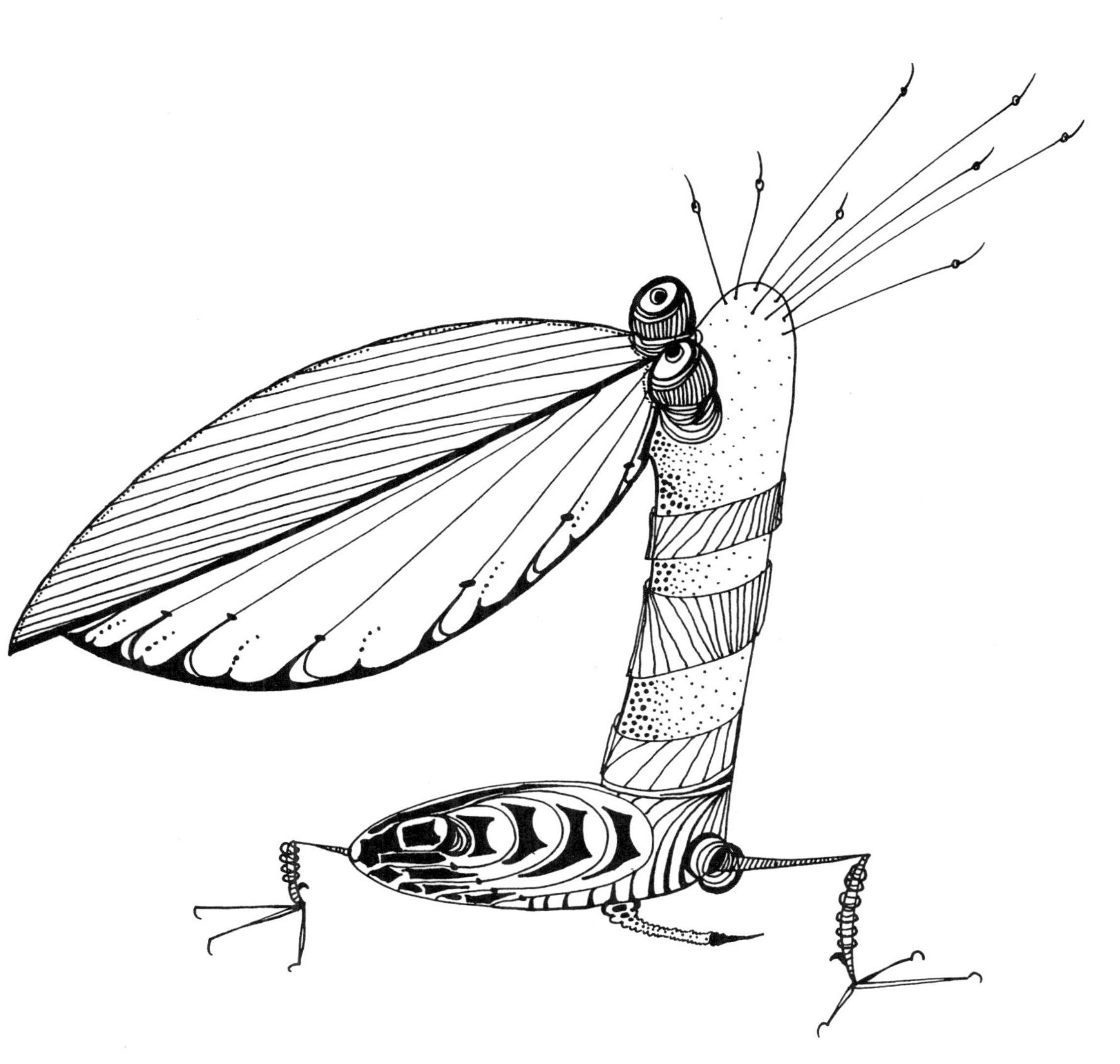

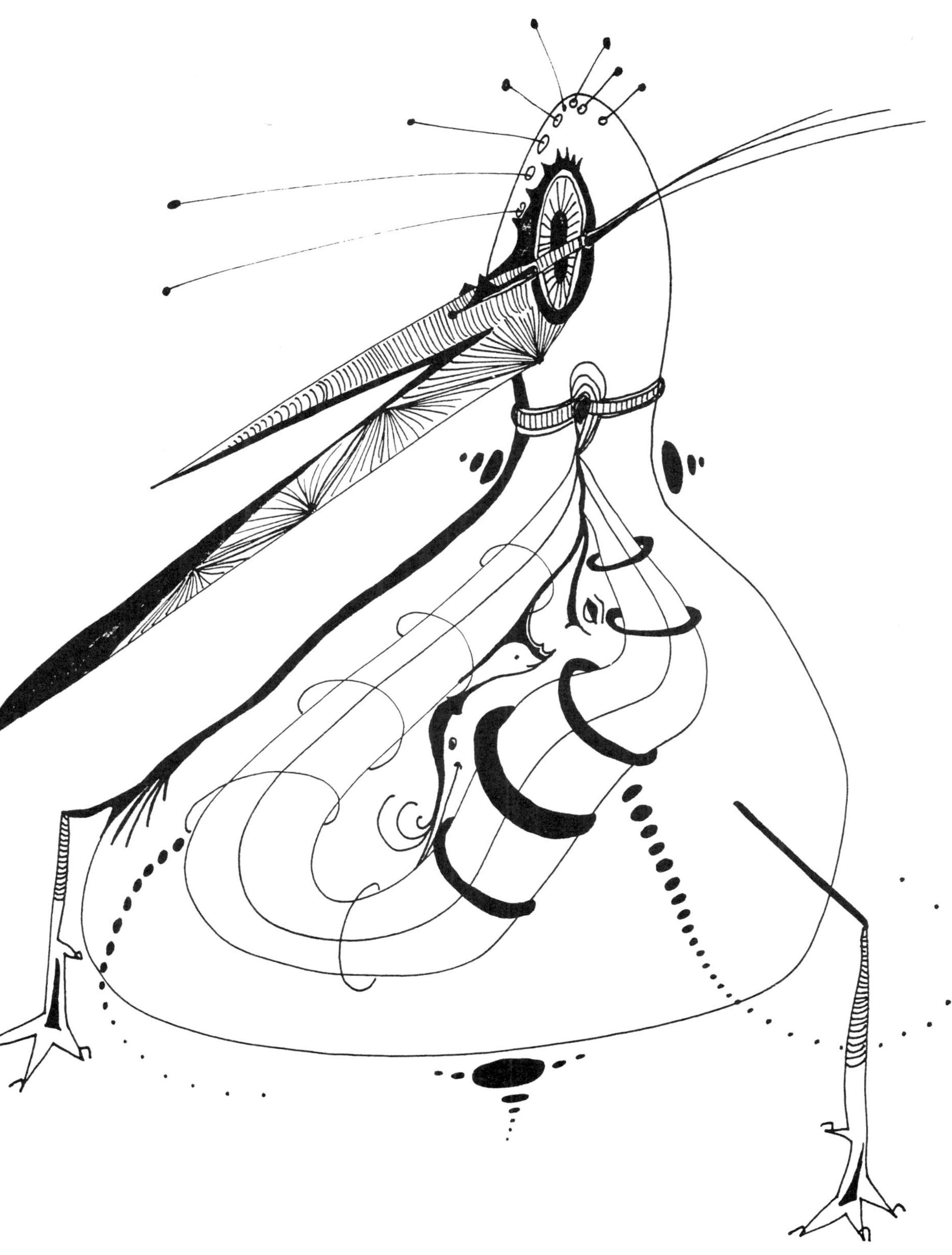

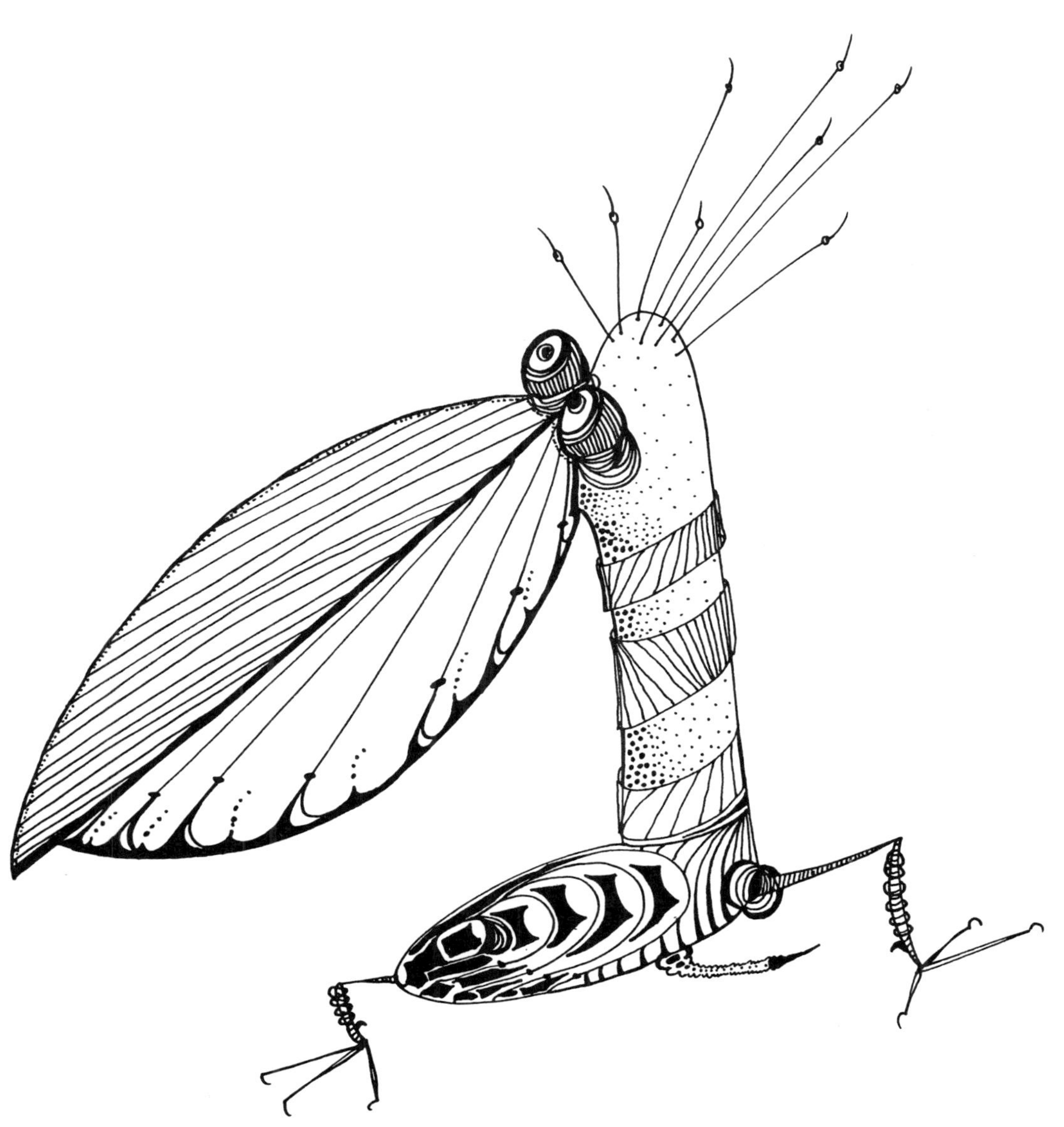

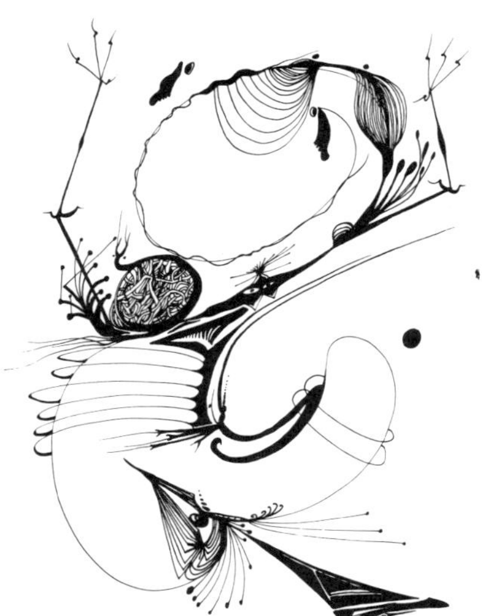

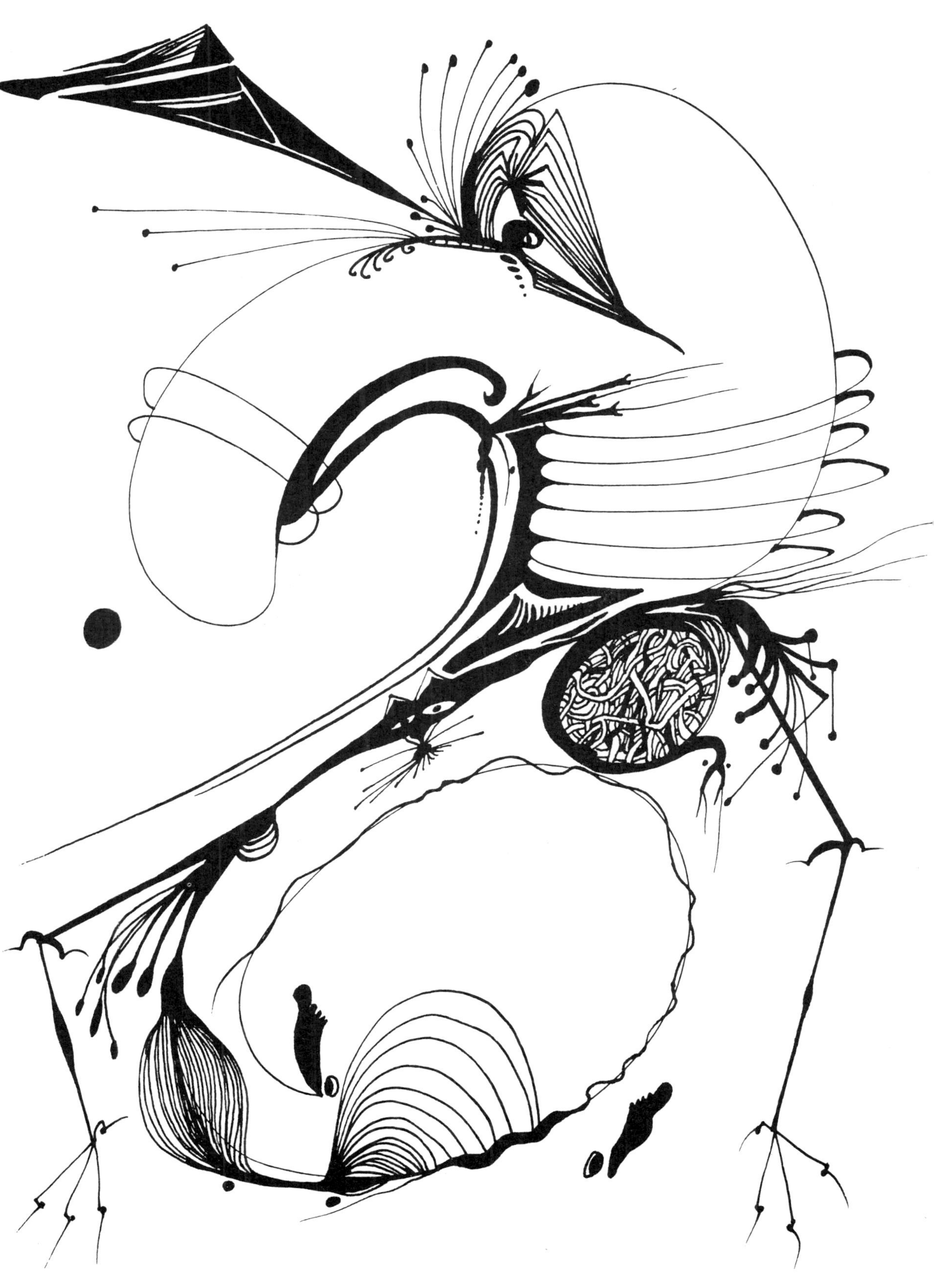

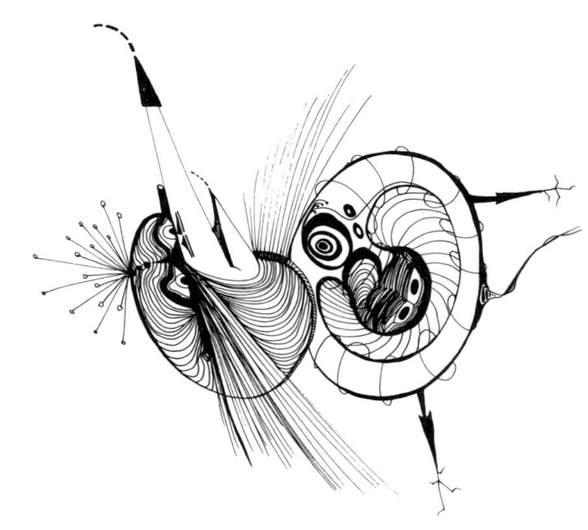

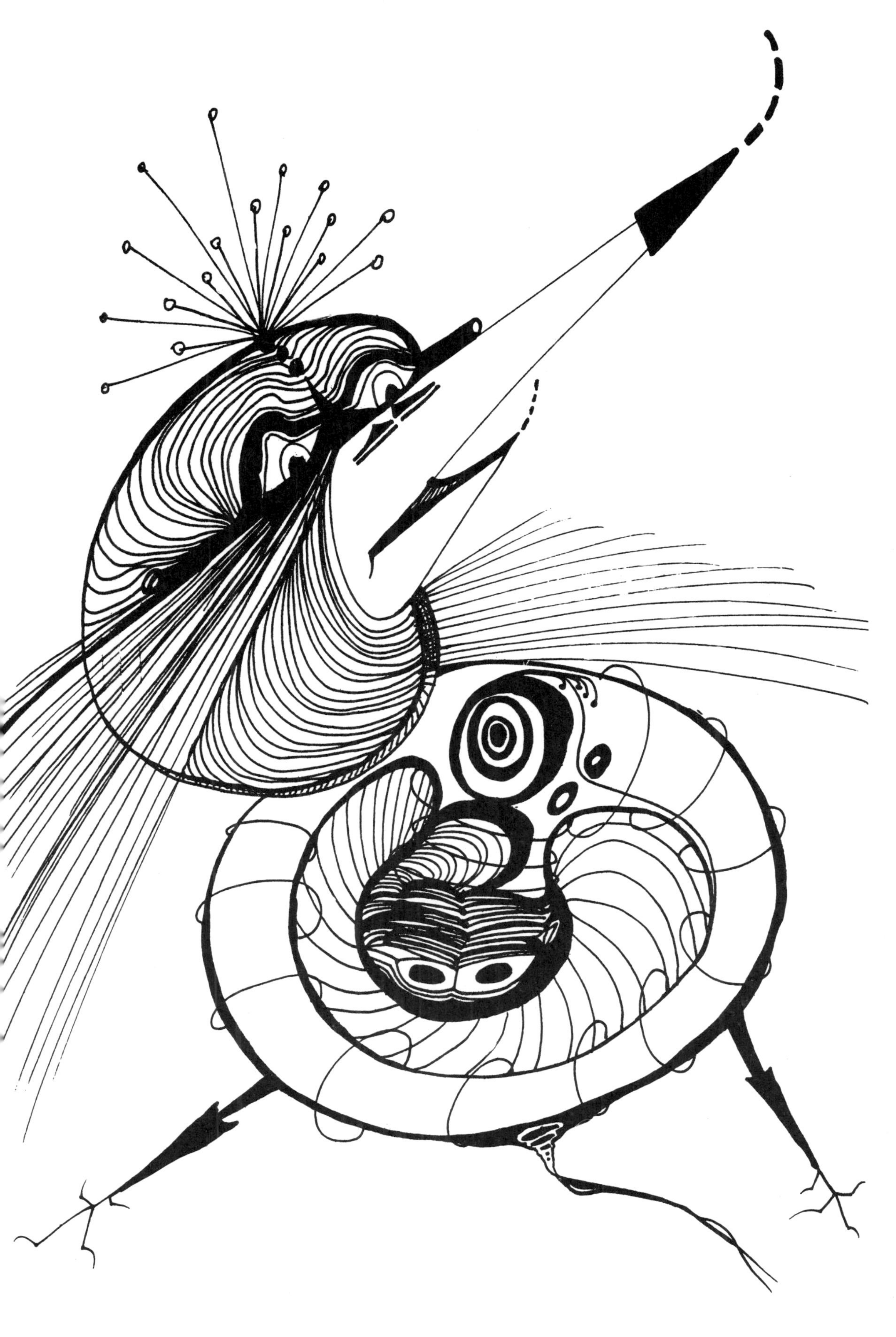

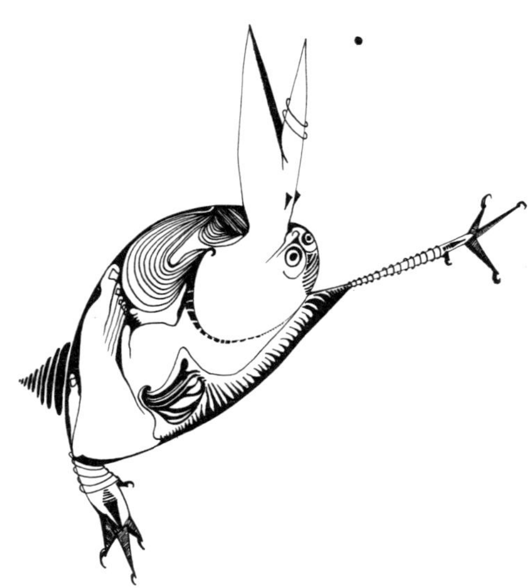

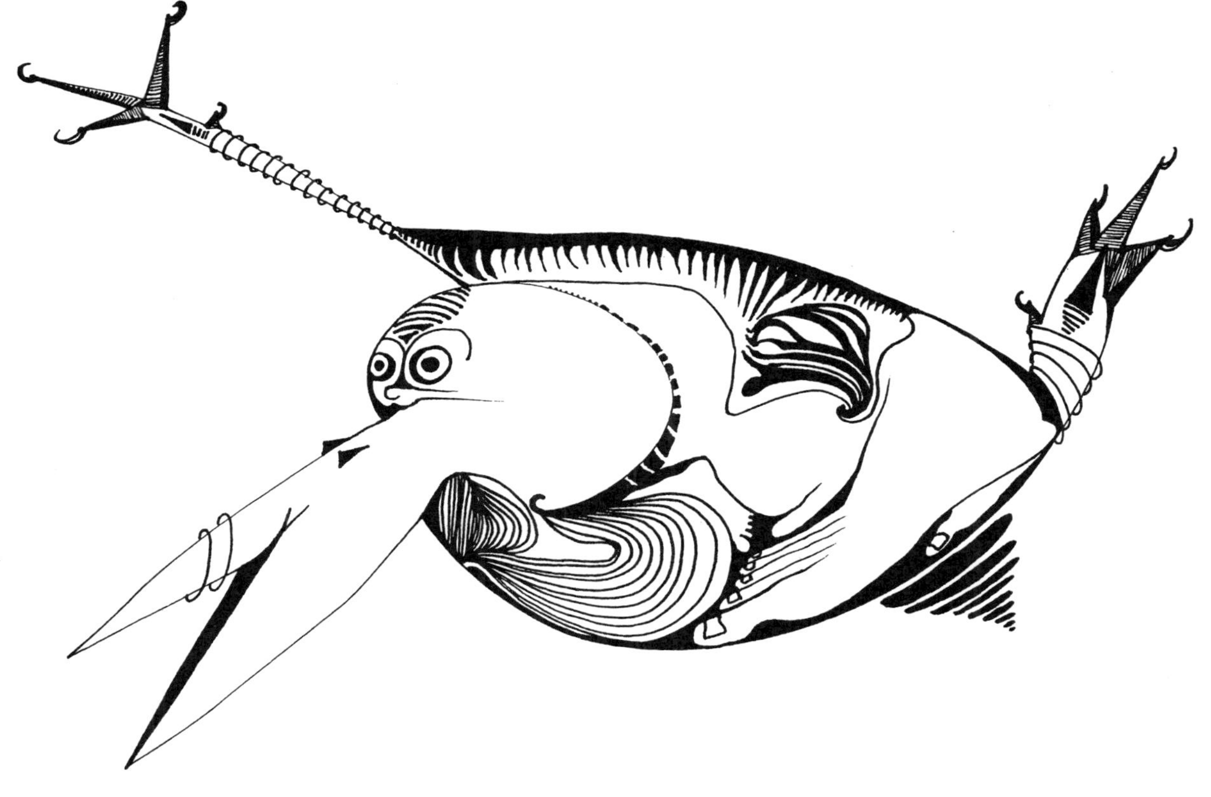

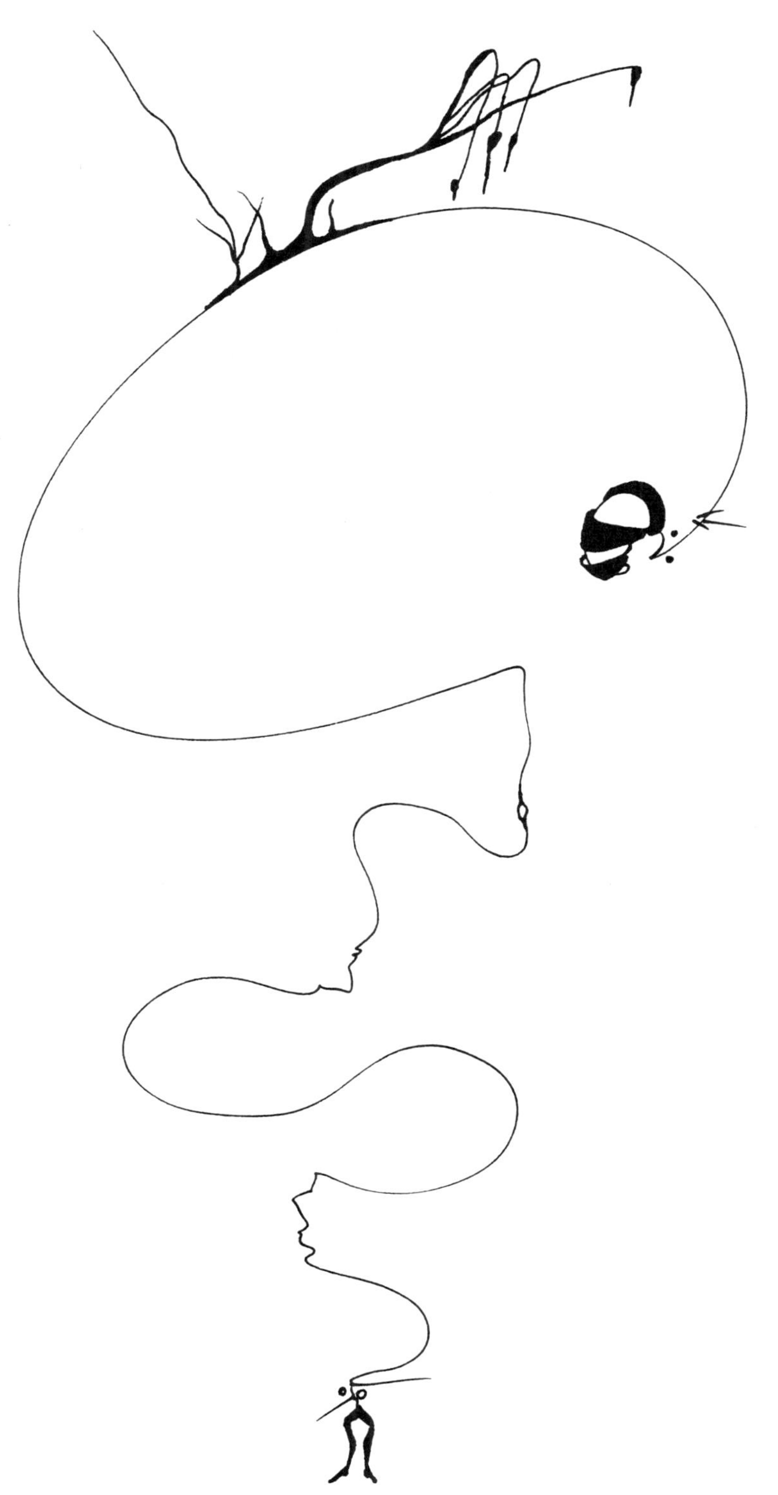

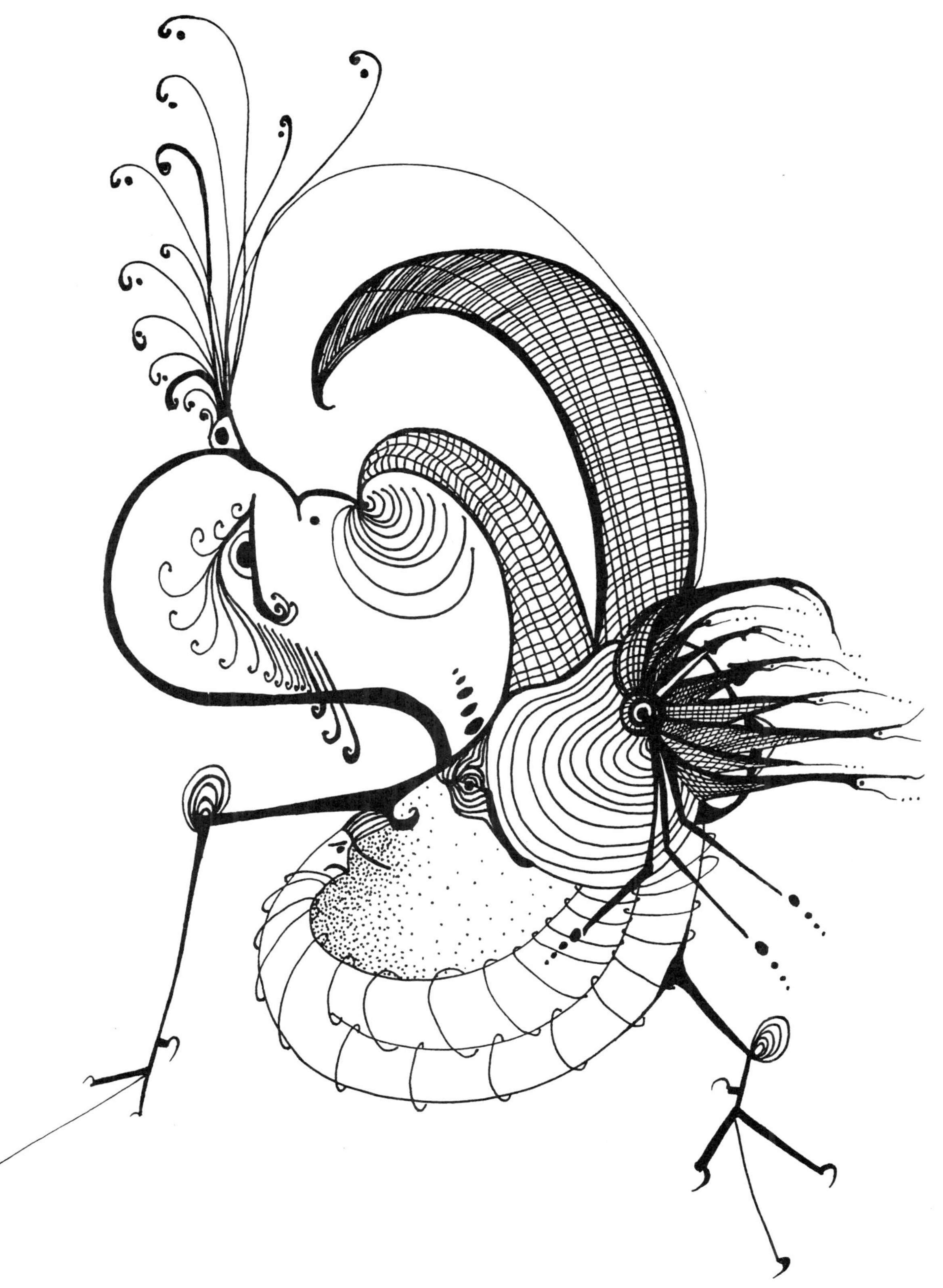

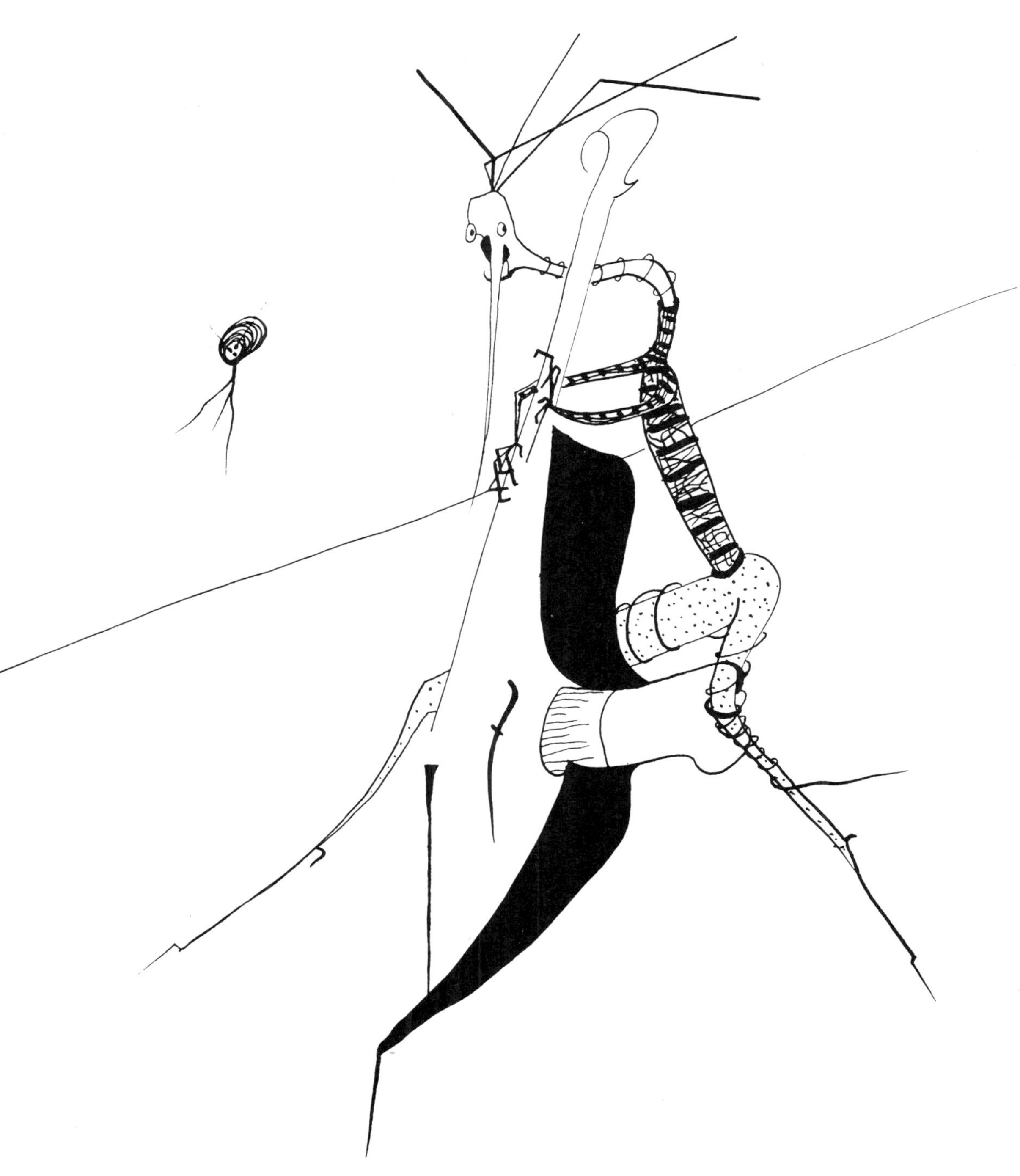

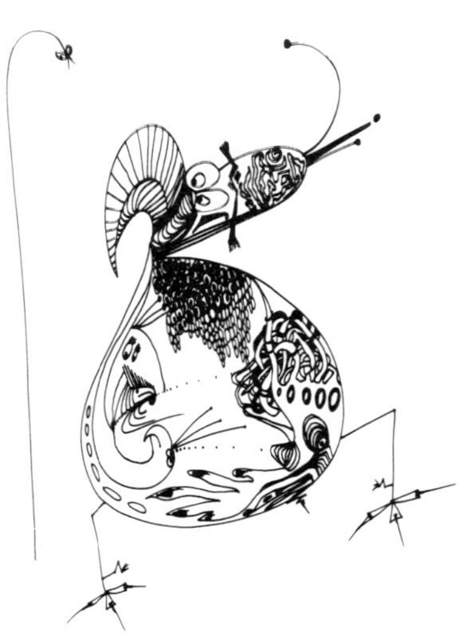

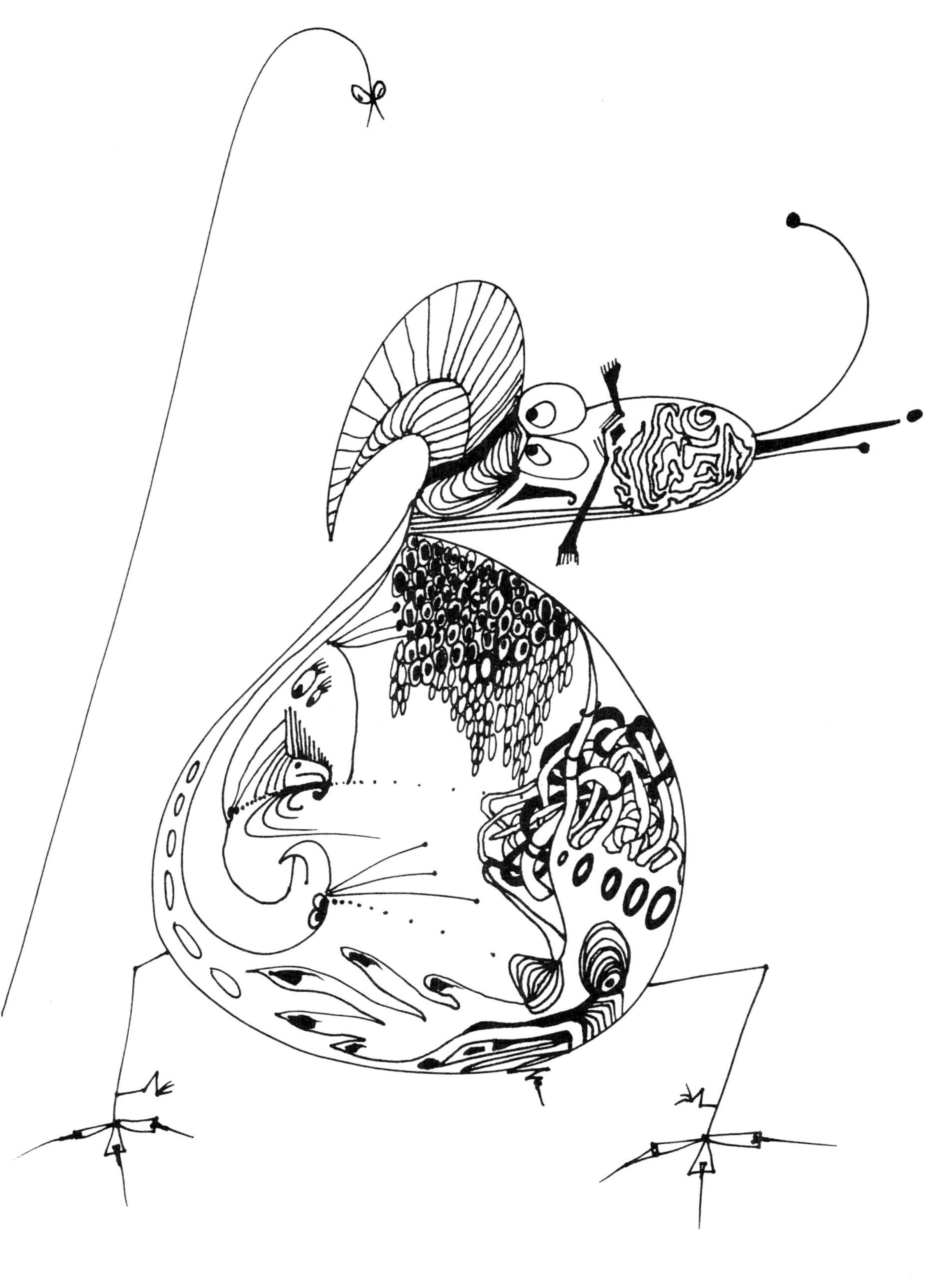

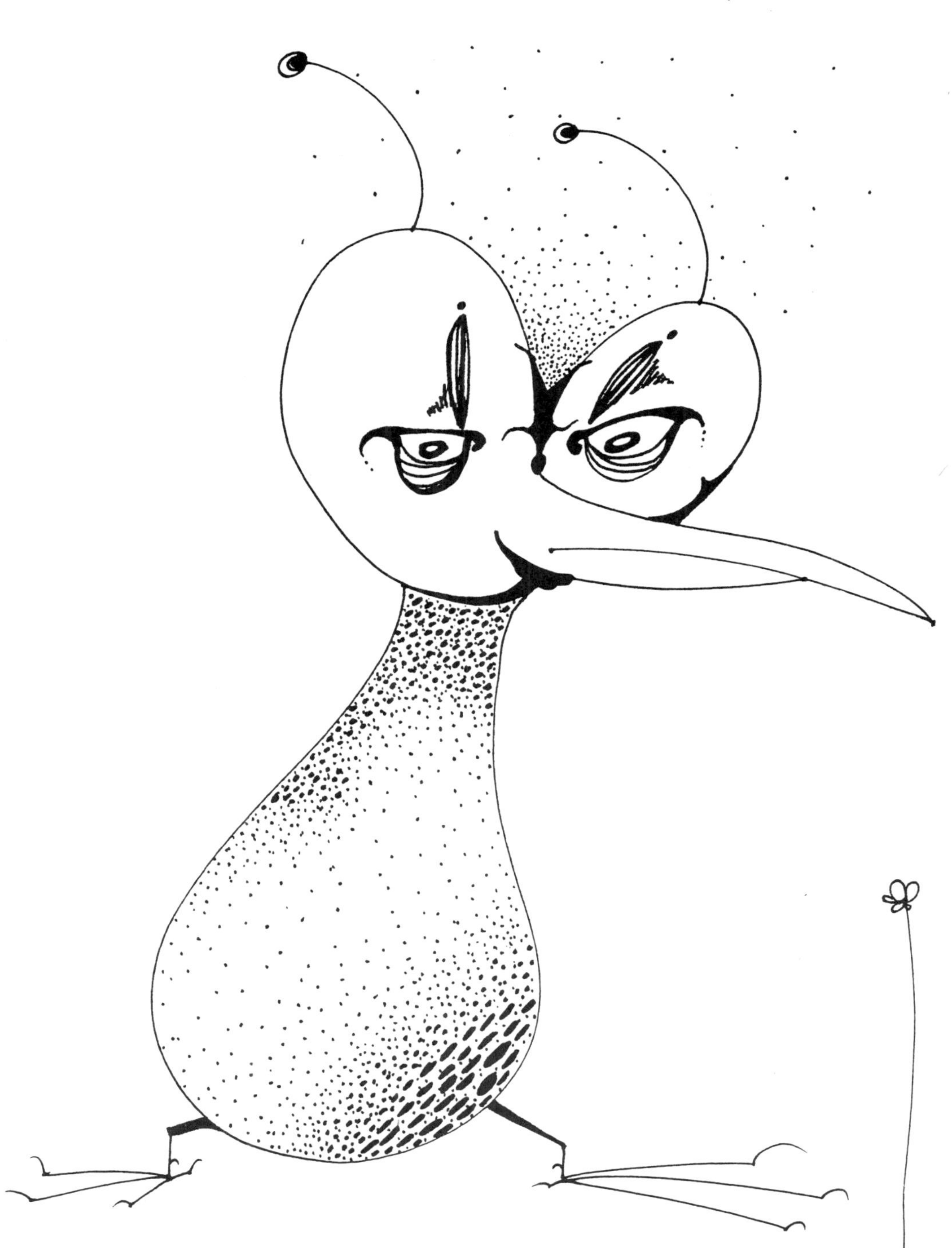

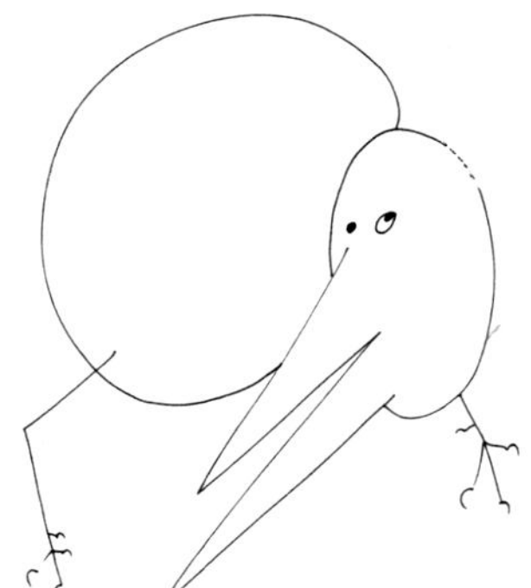

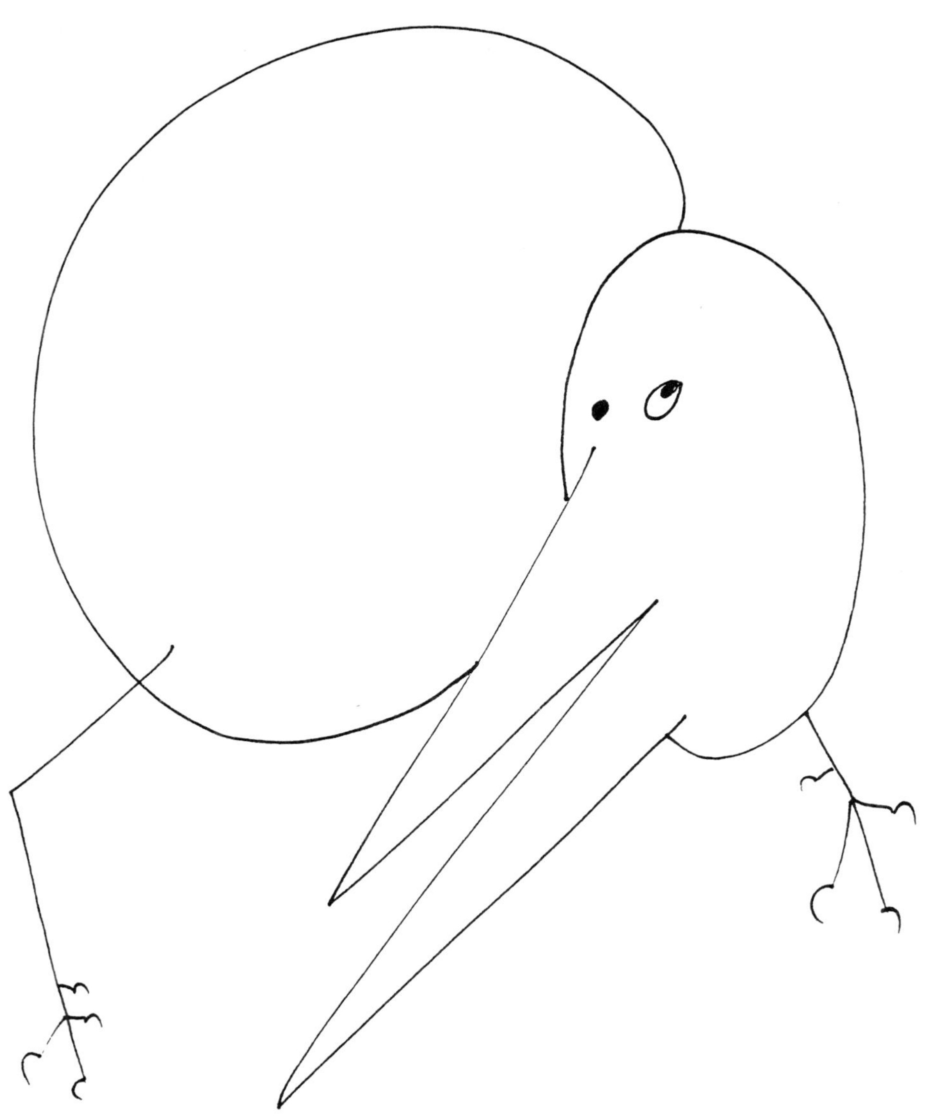

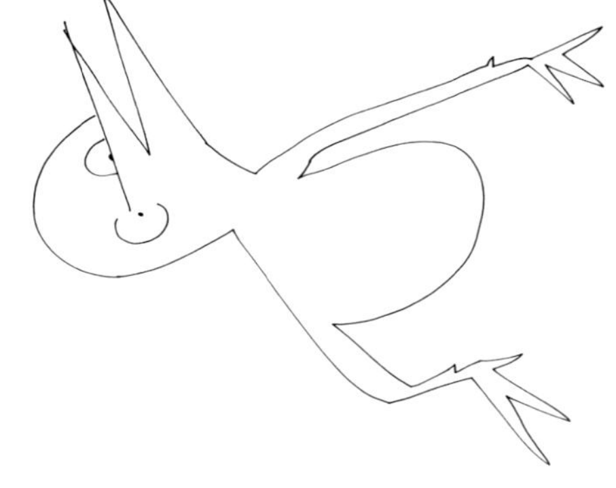

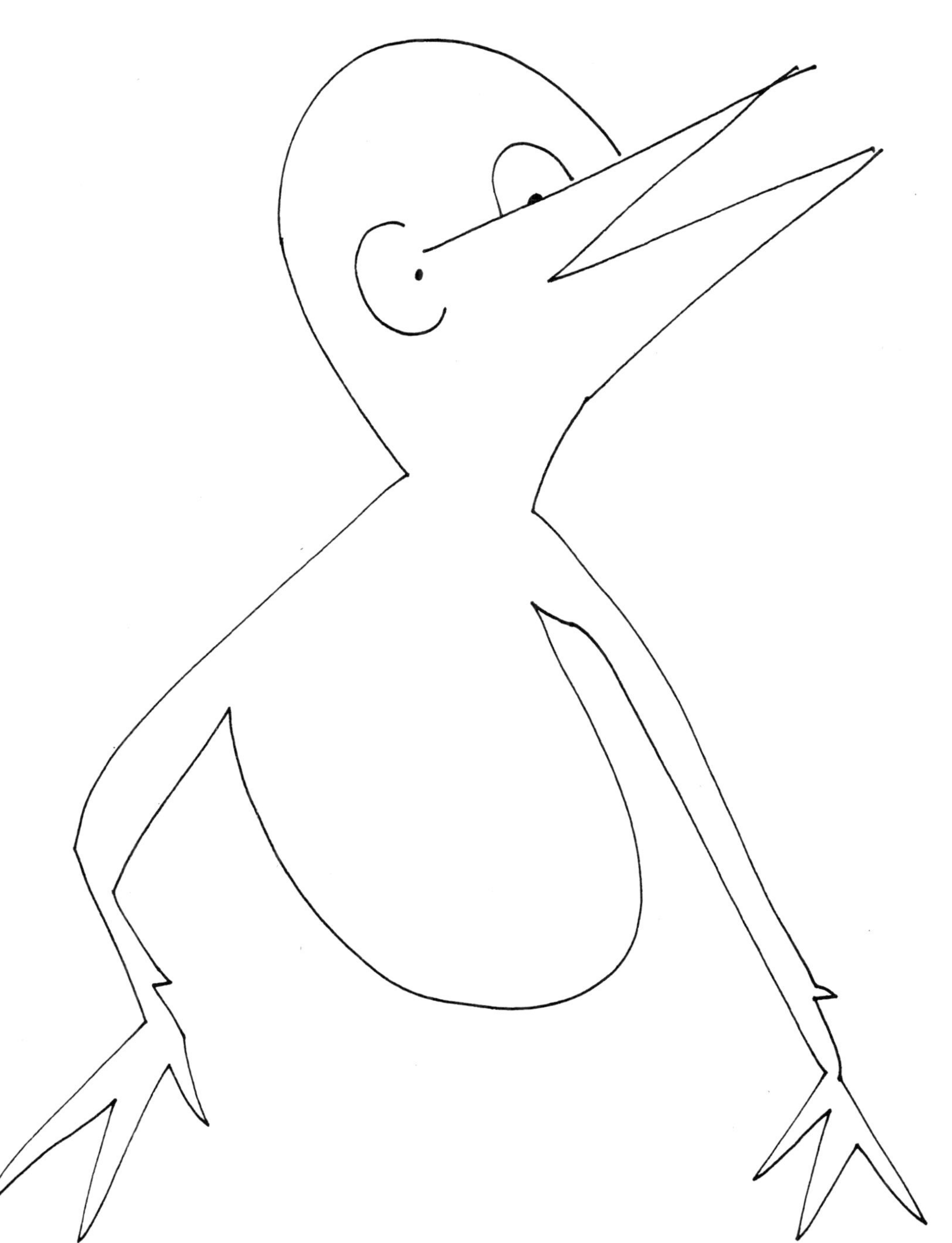

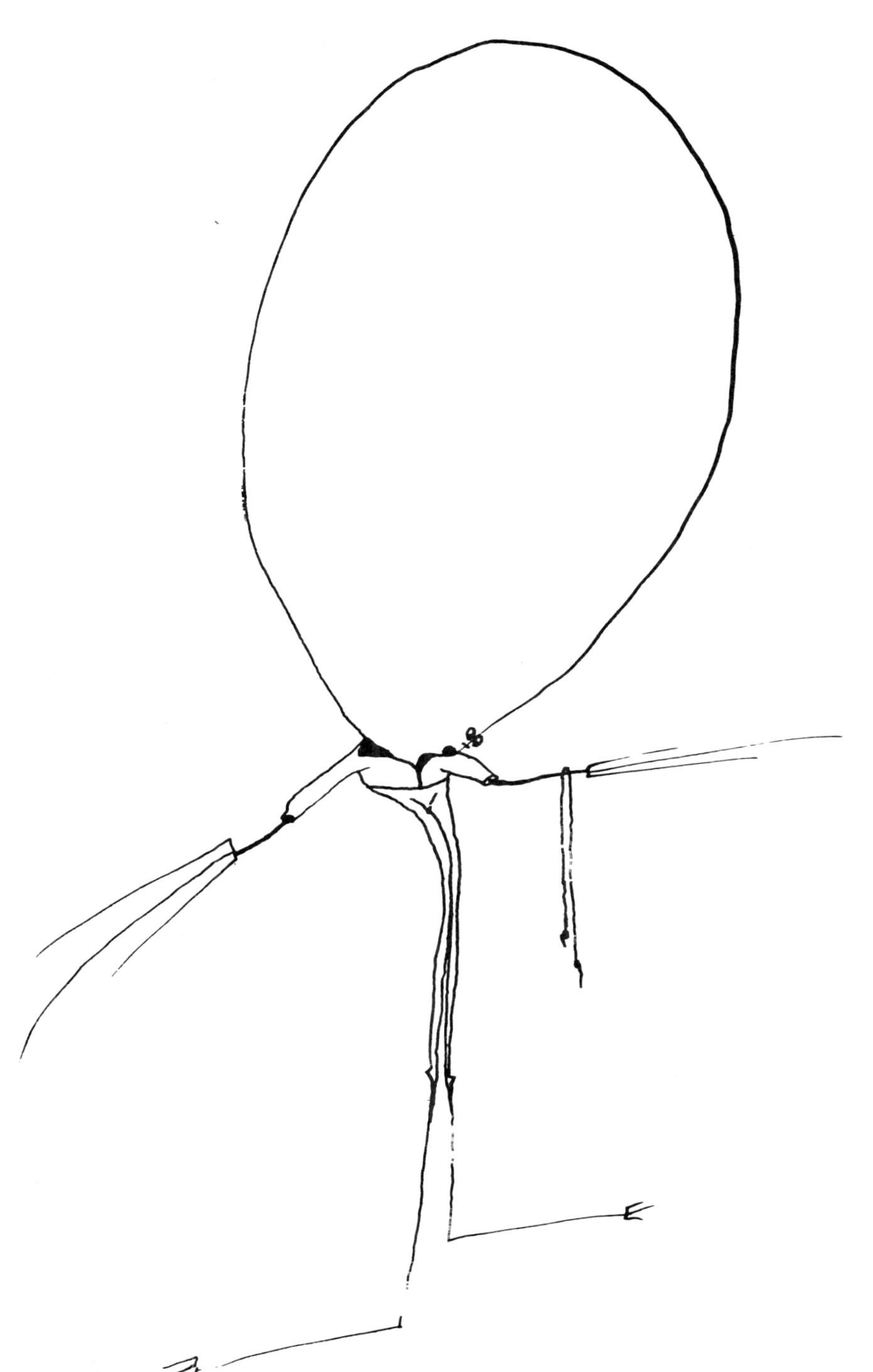

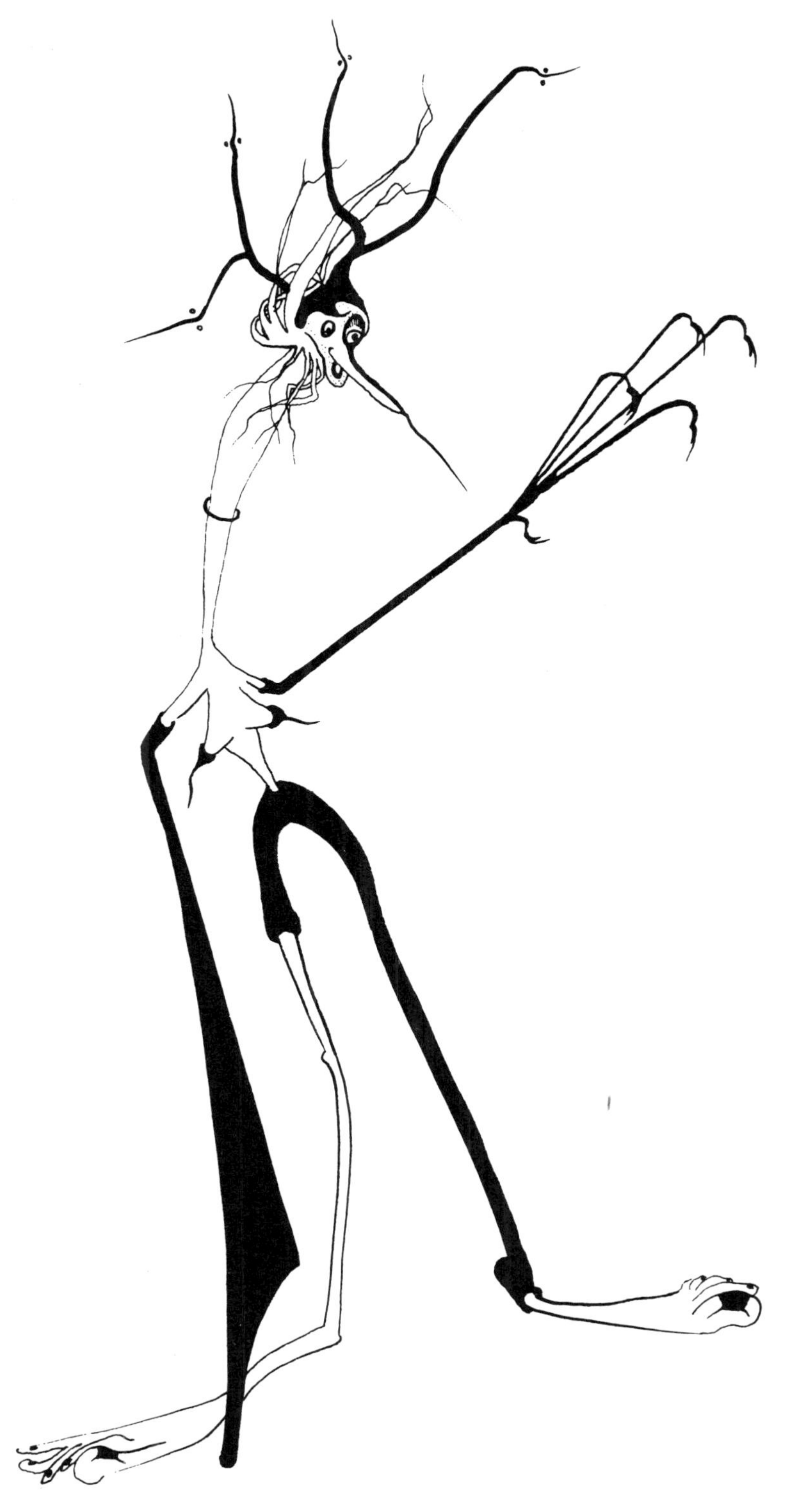

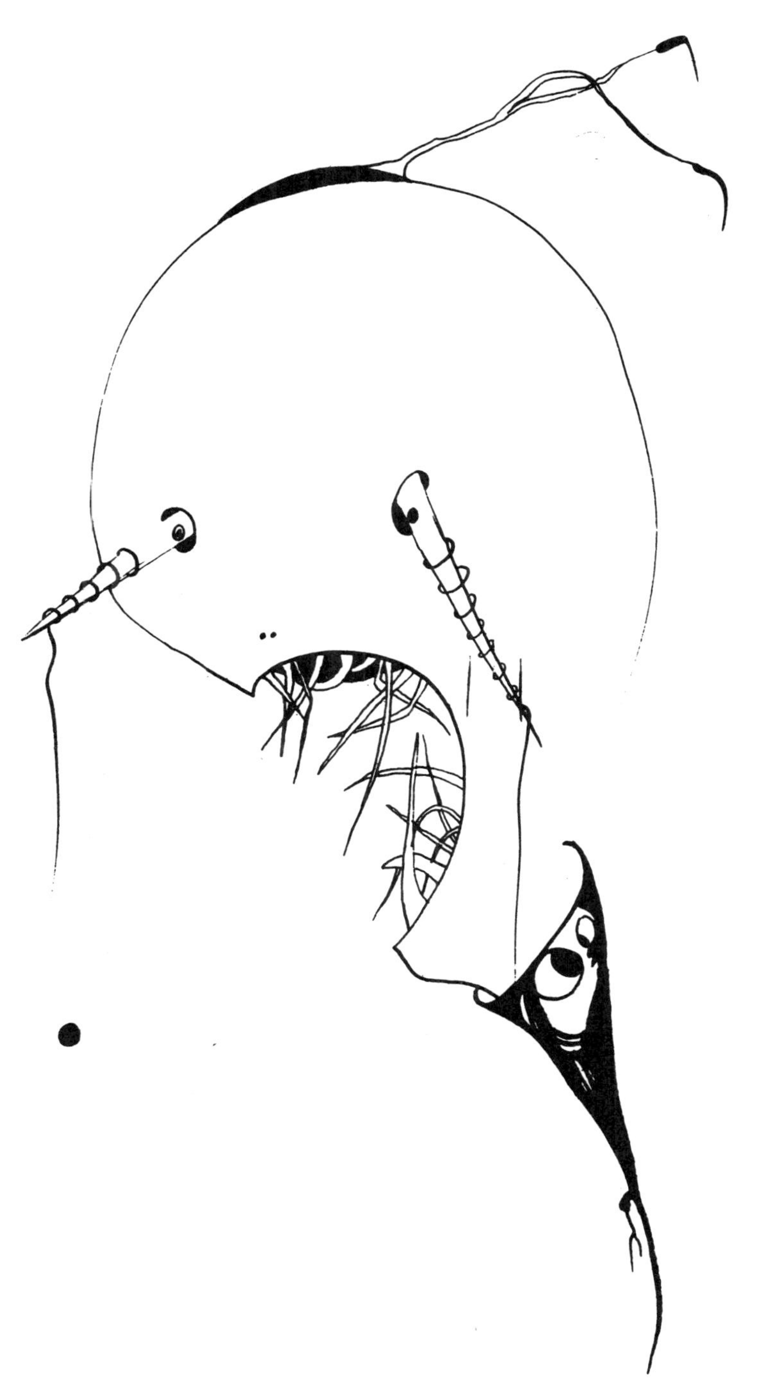

CHAMBER ENSEMBLES

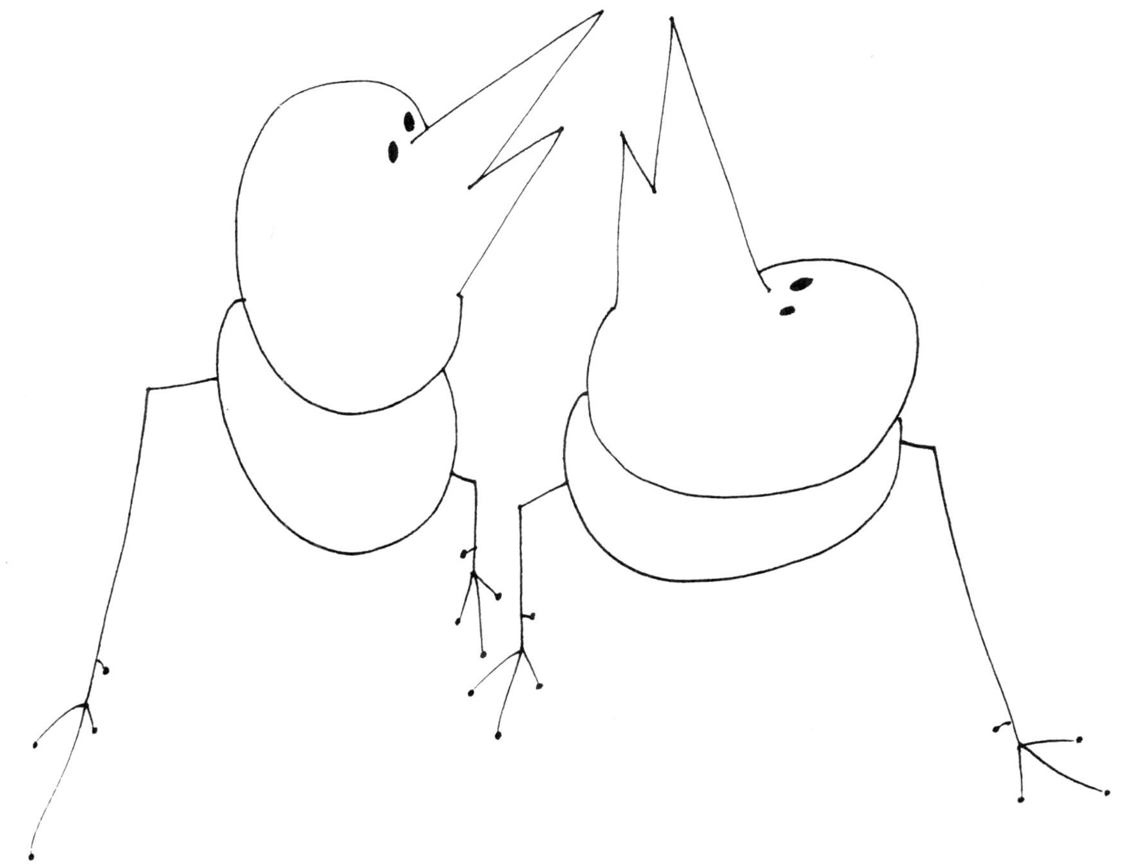

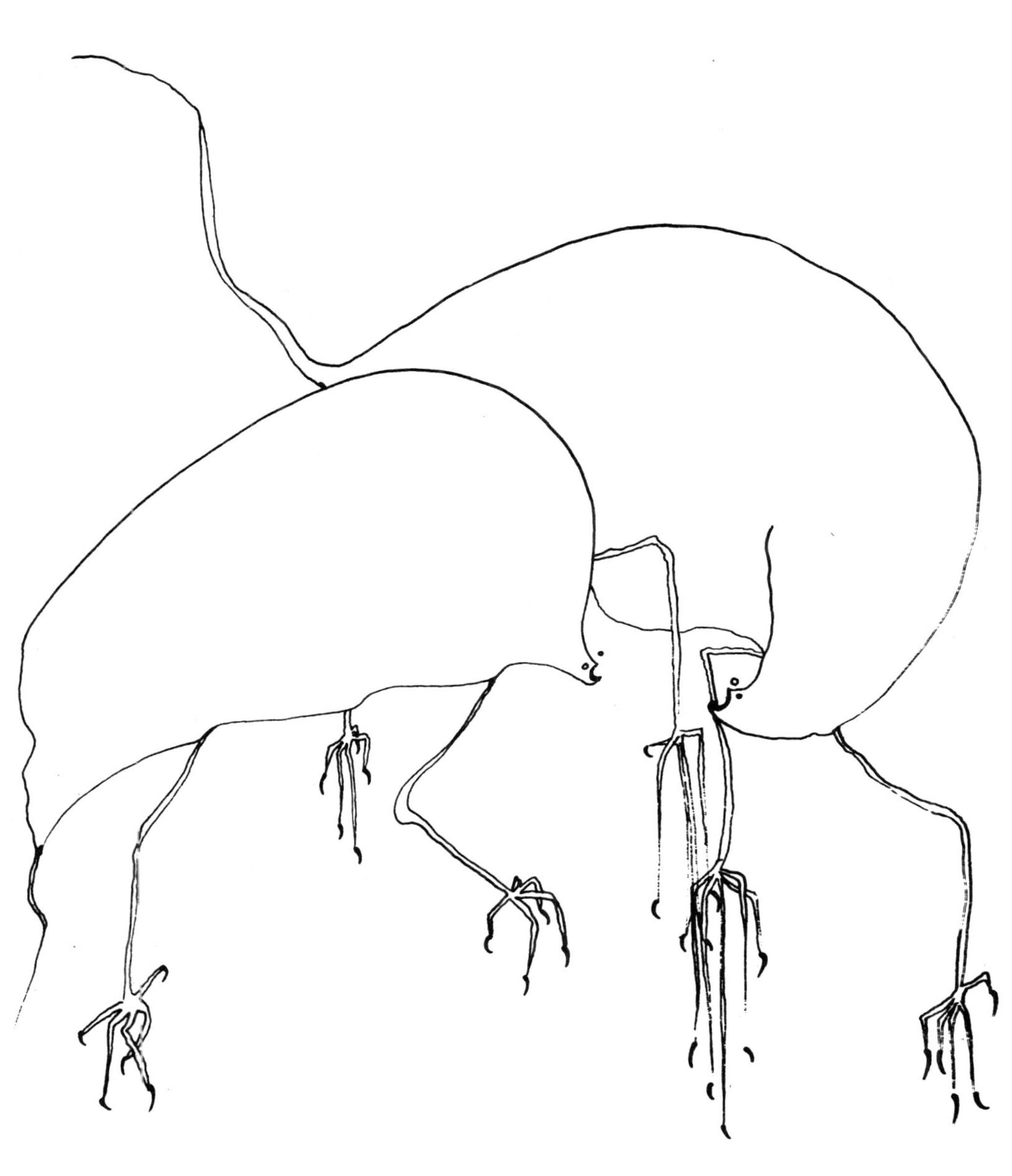

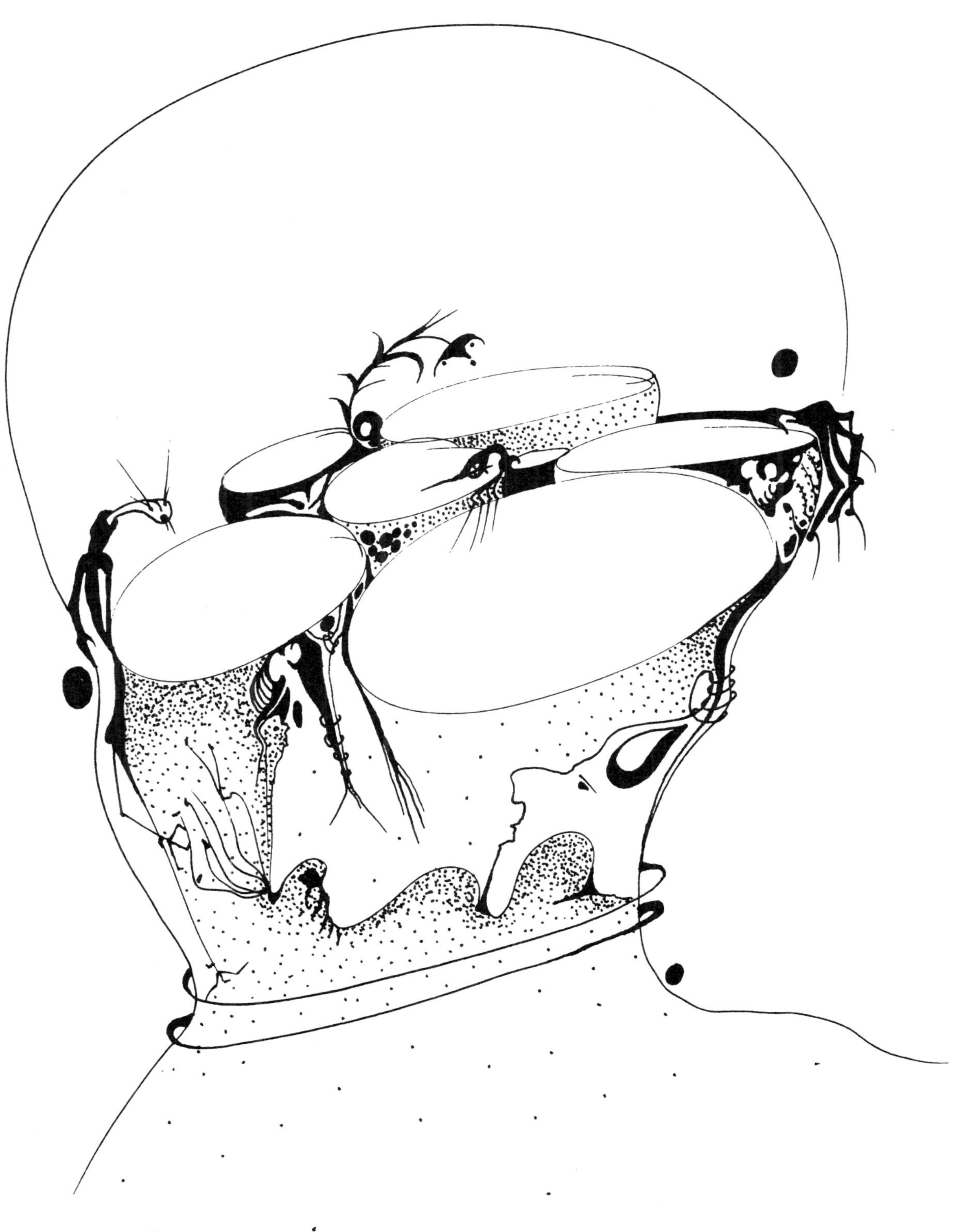

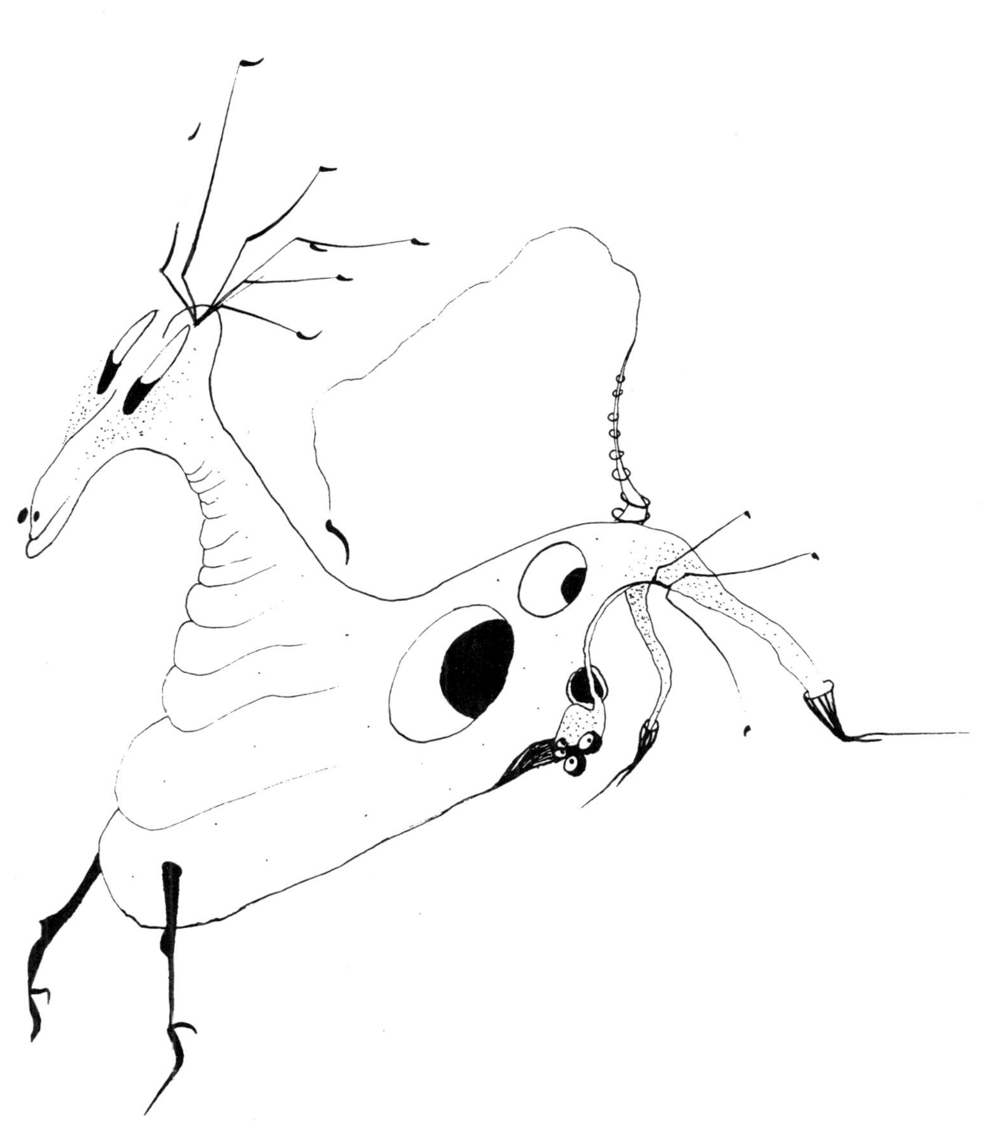

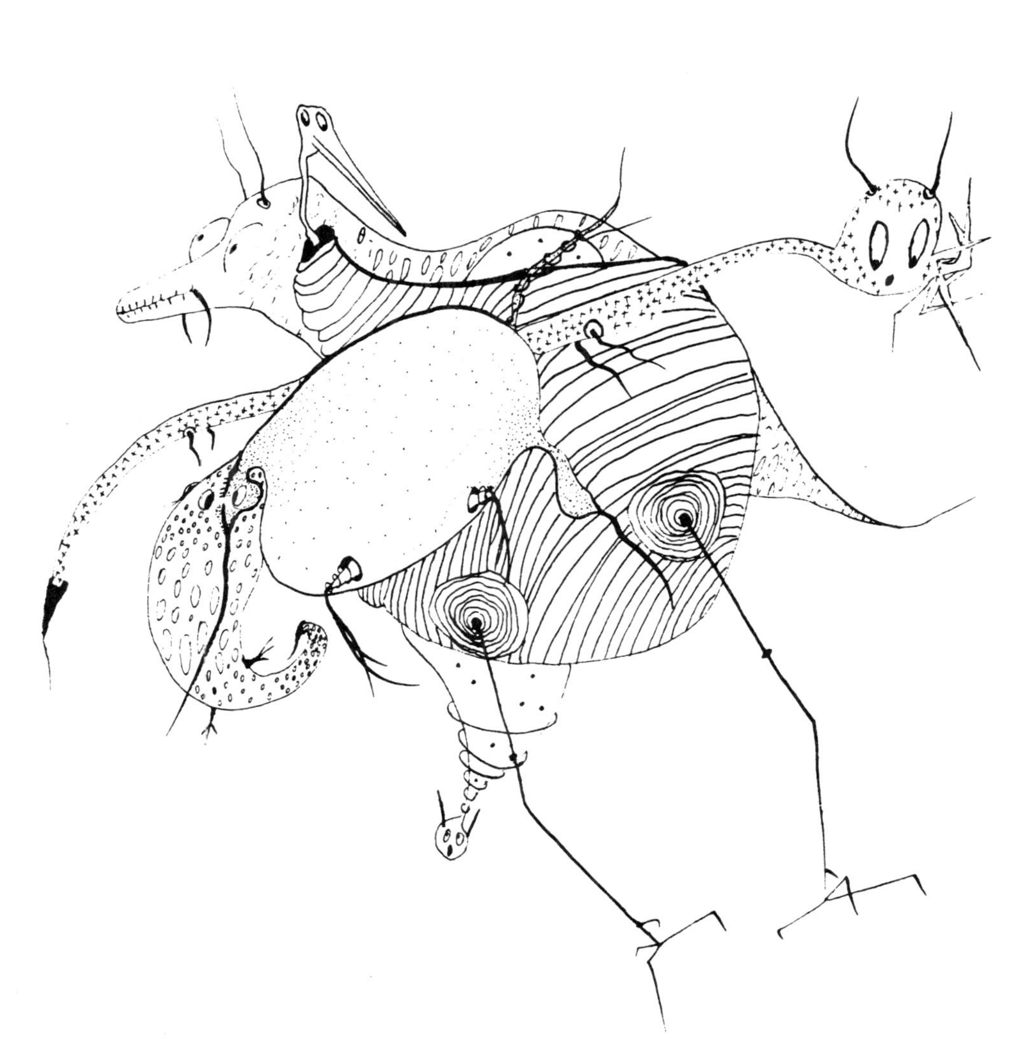

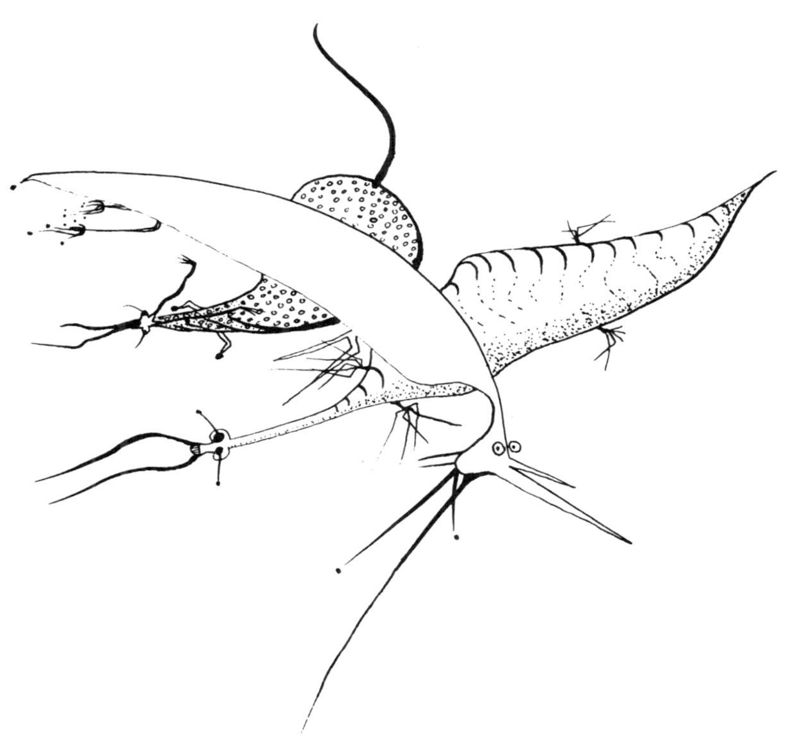

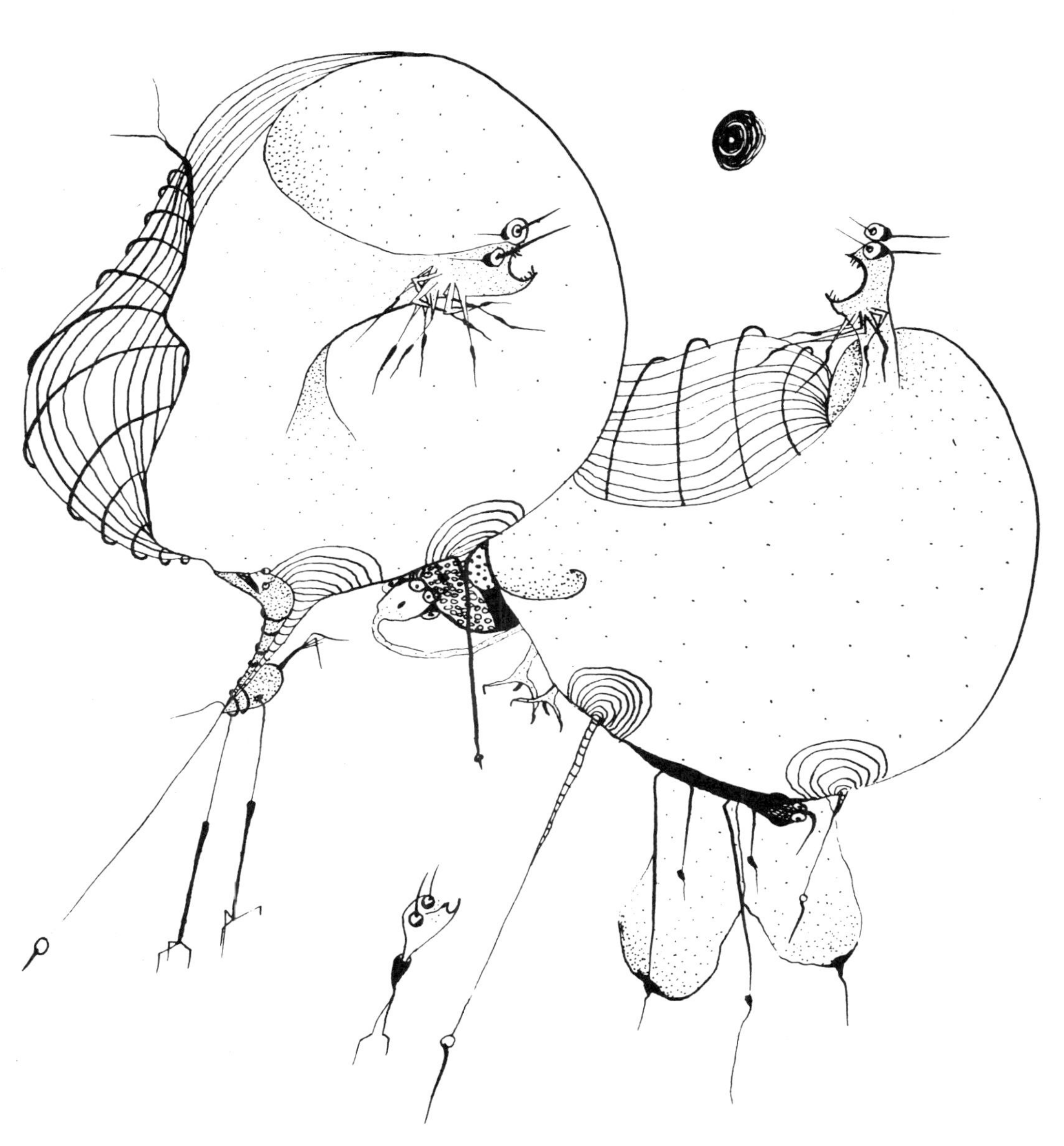

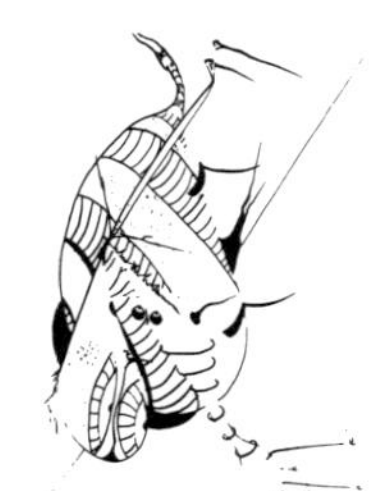

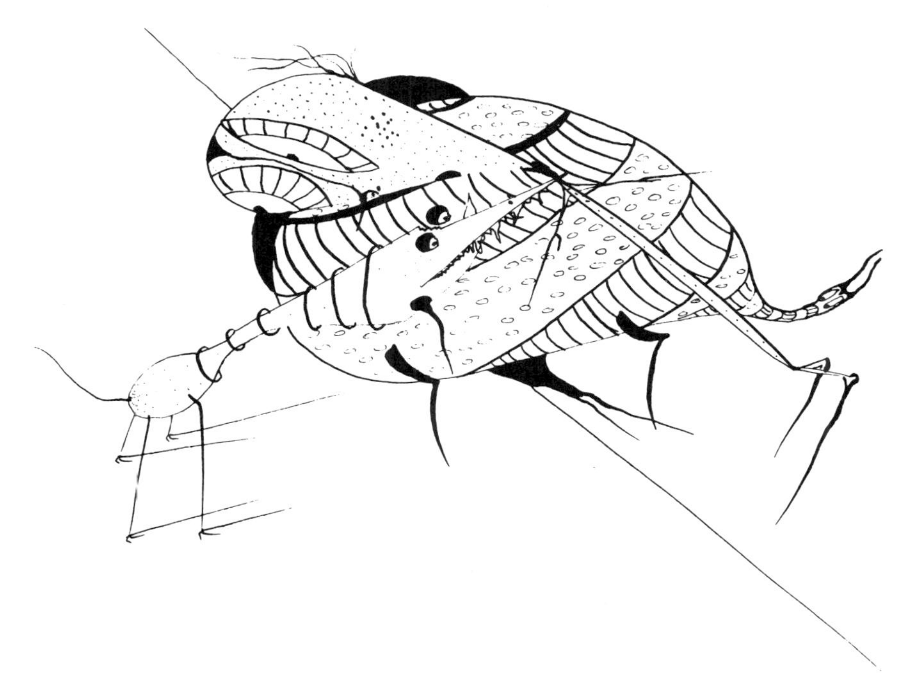

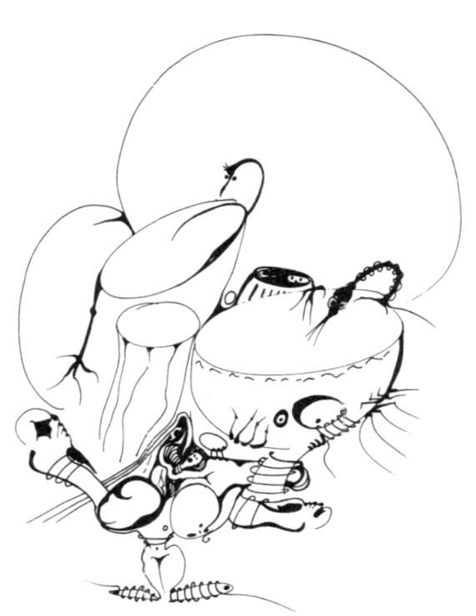

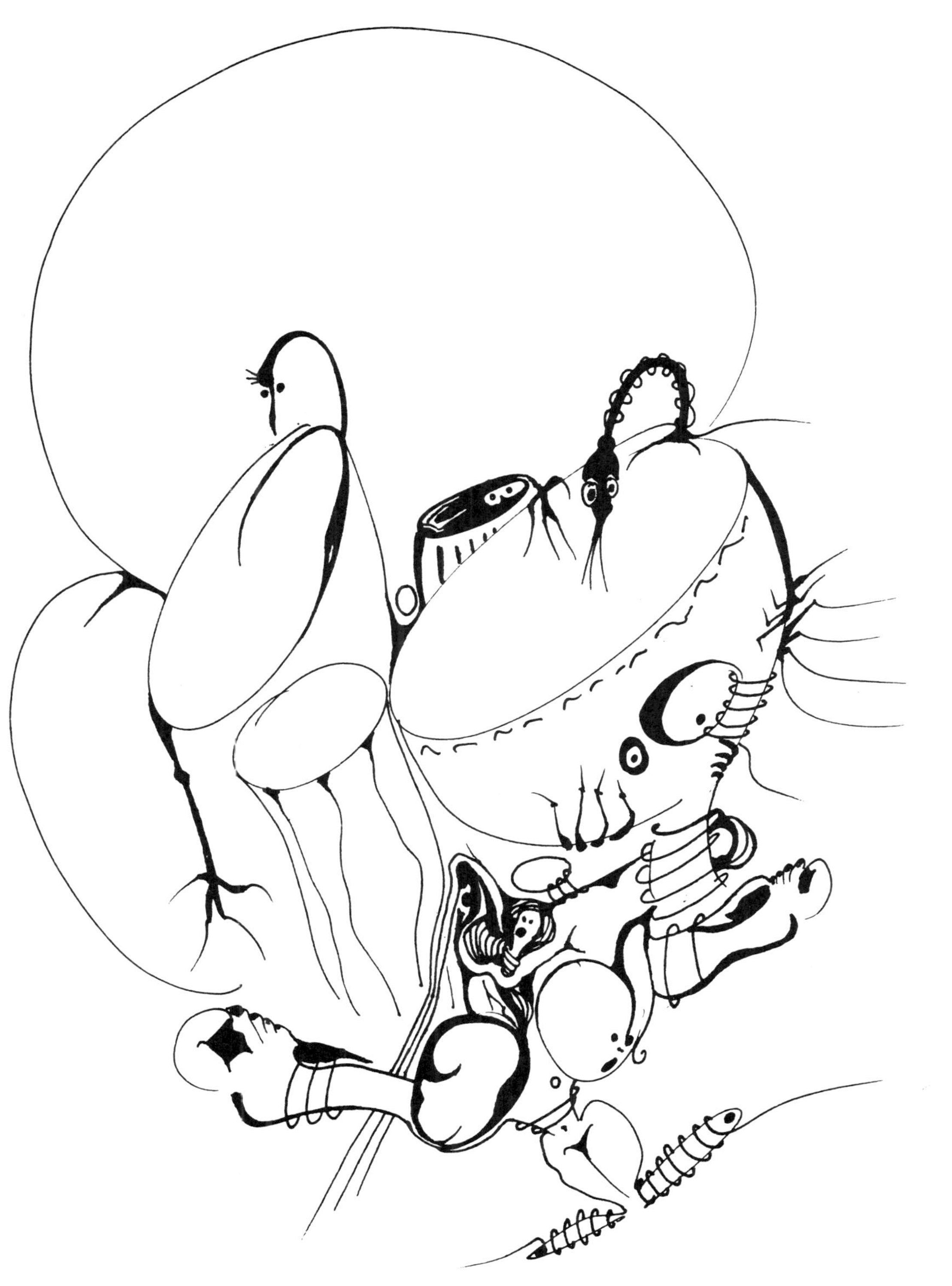

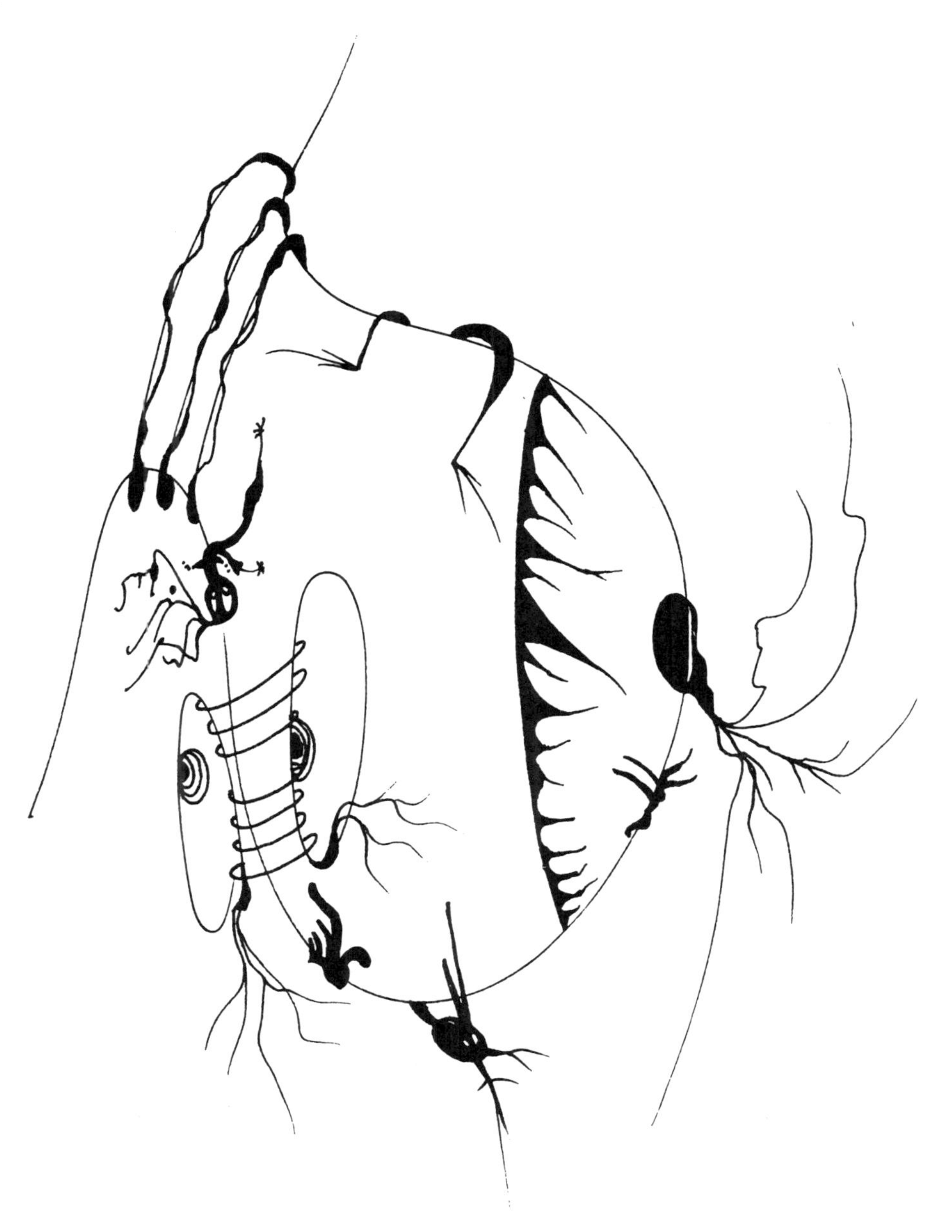

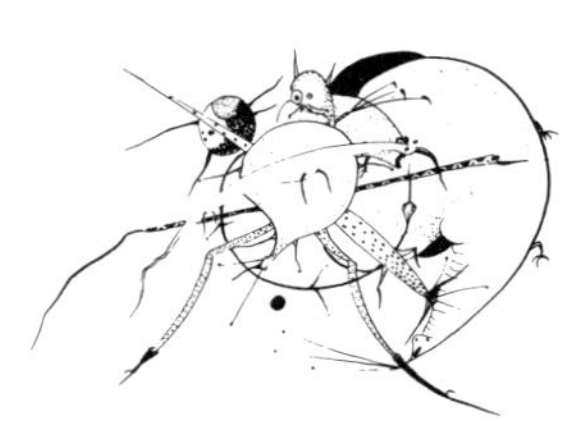

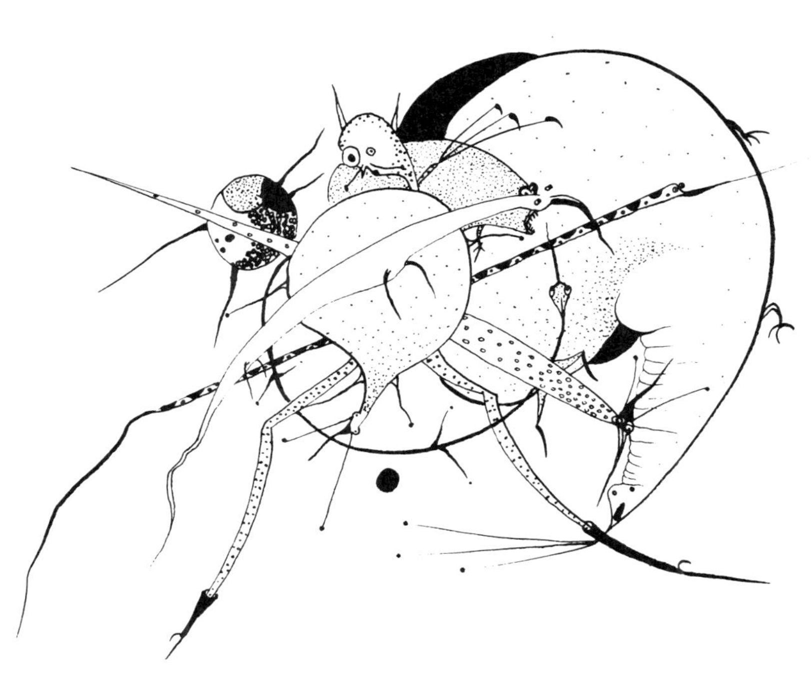

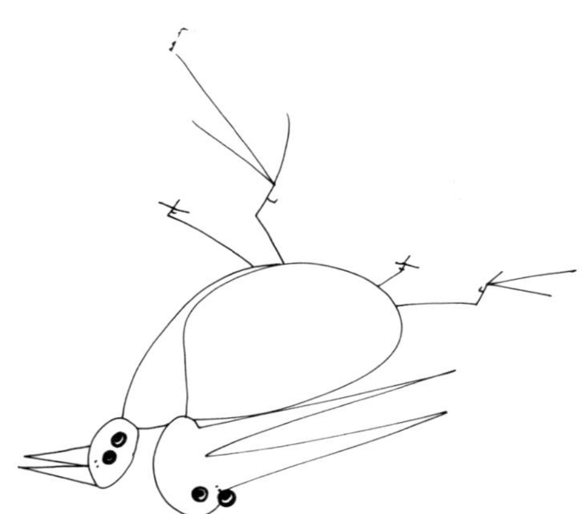

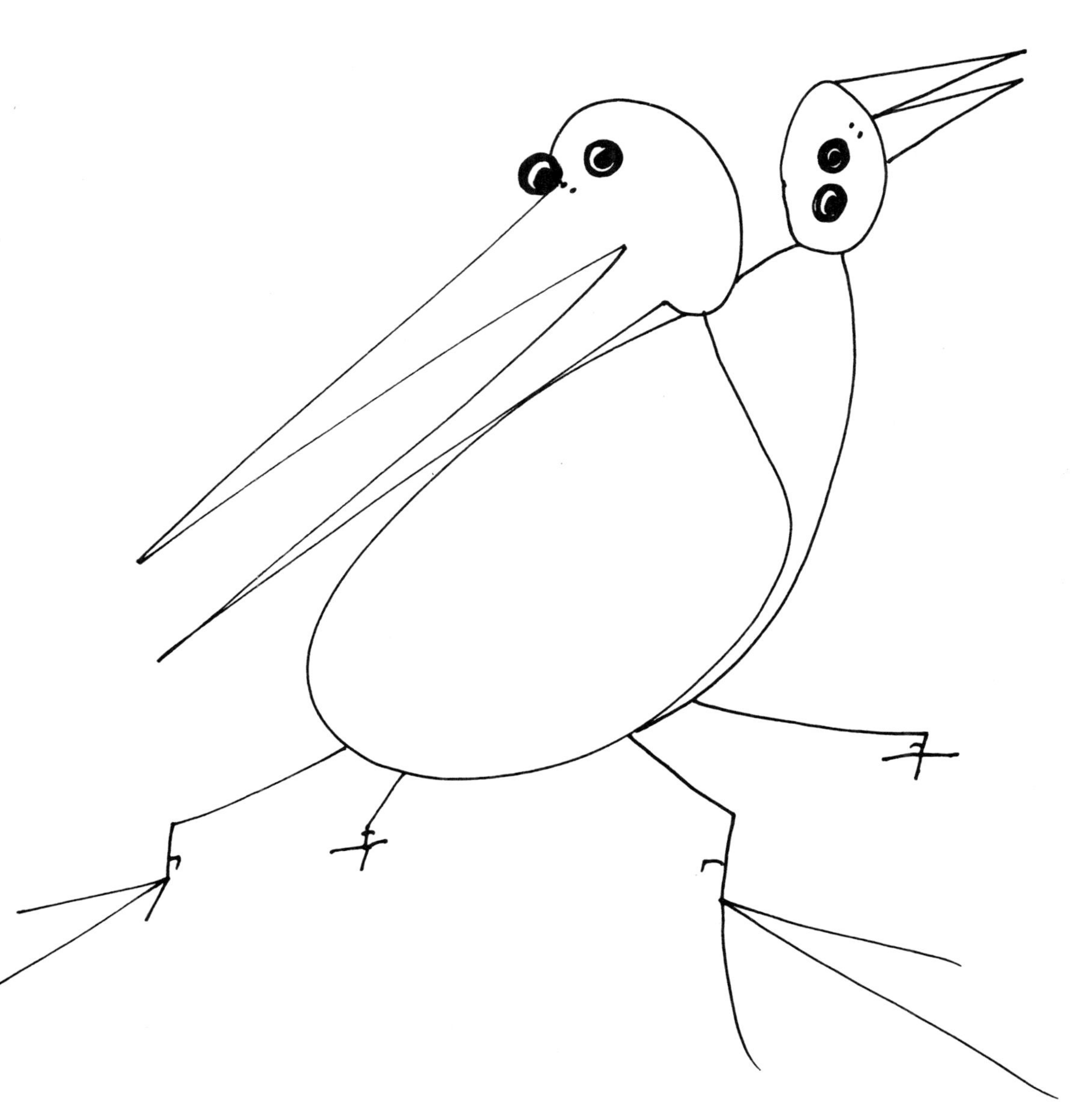

CHAMBER ORCHESTRAS

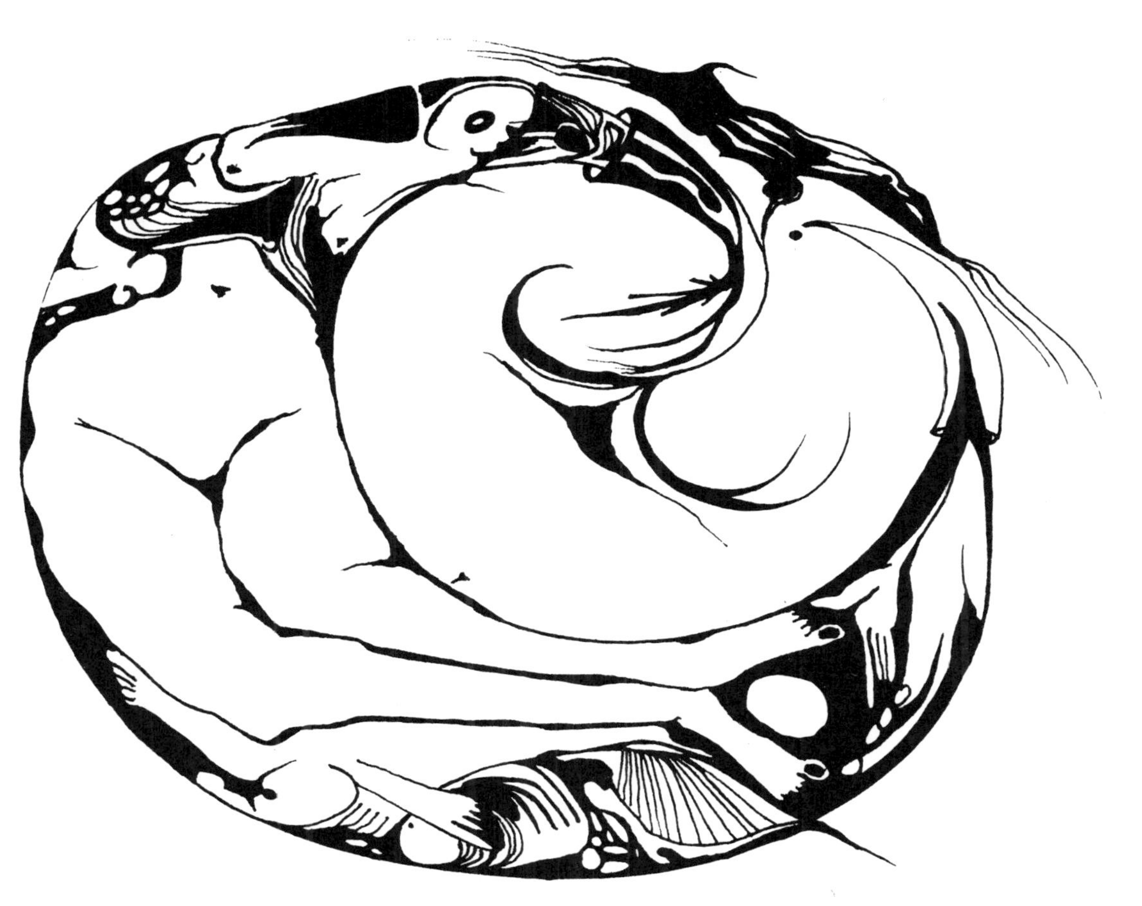

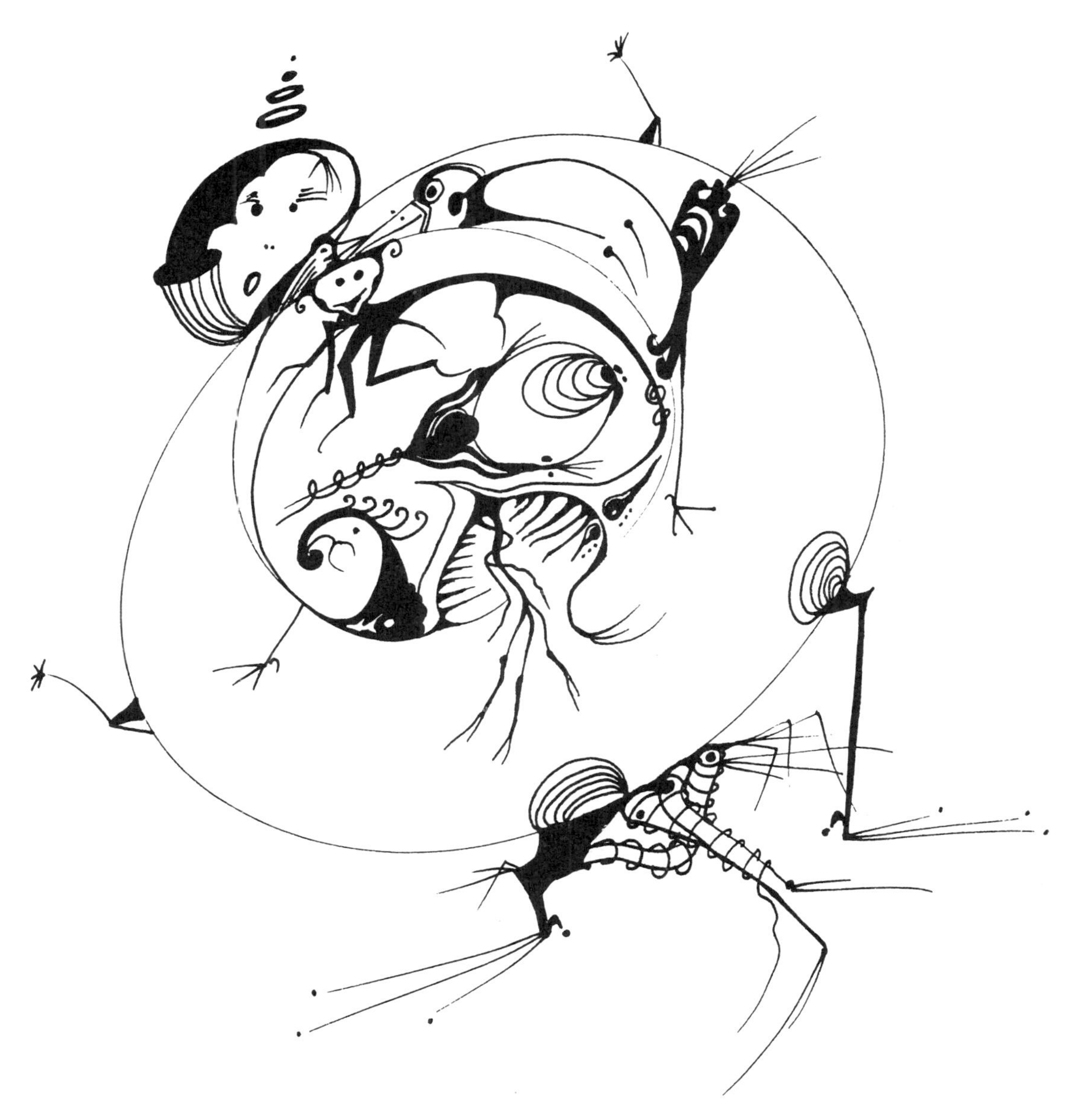

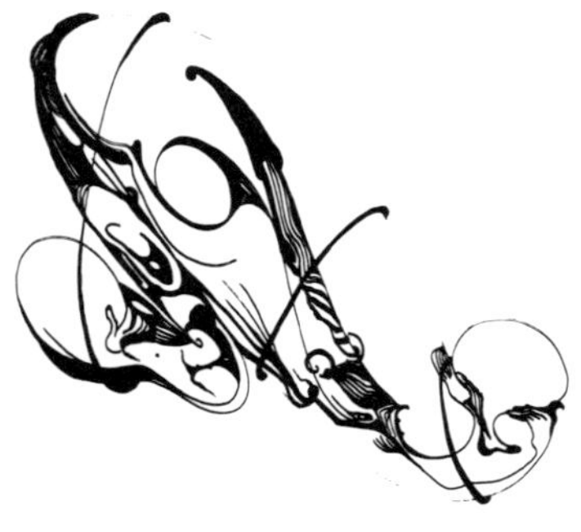

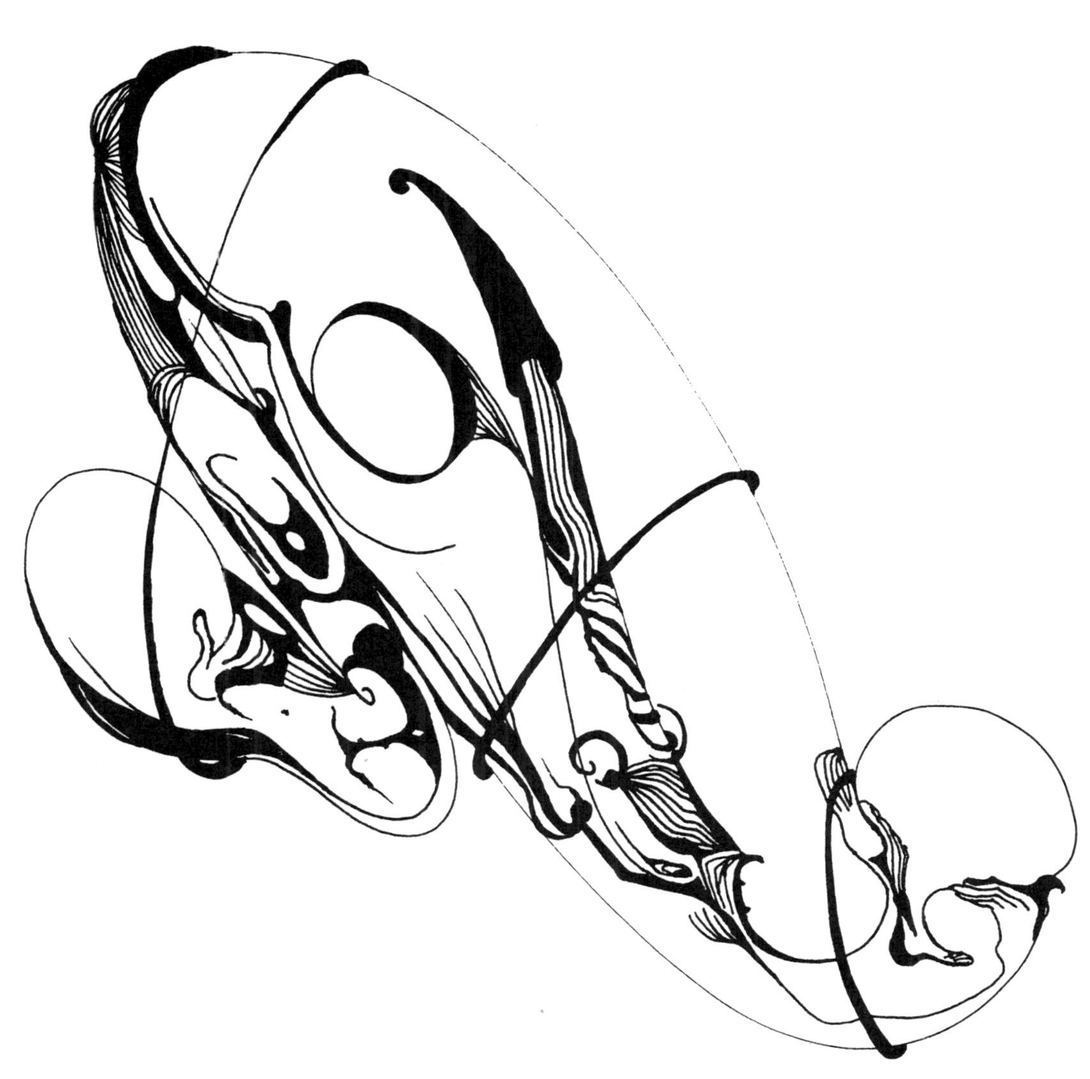

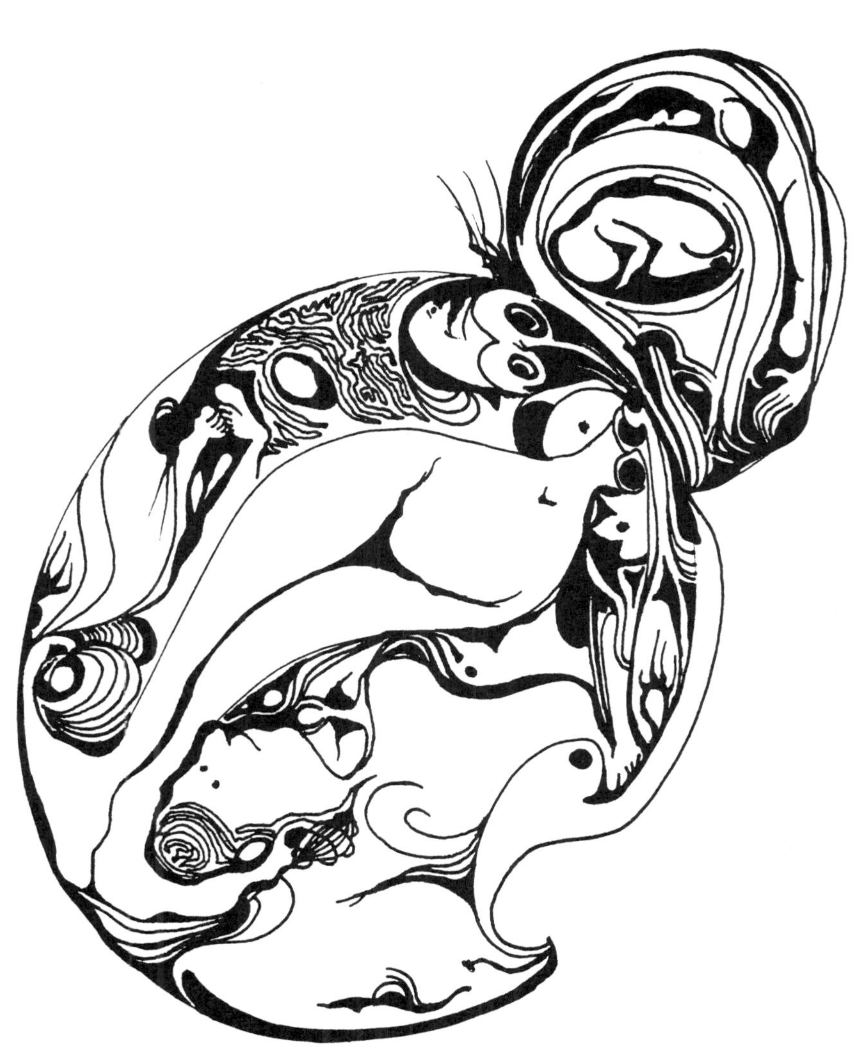

SYMPHONY ORCHESTRAS

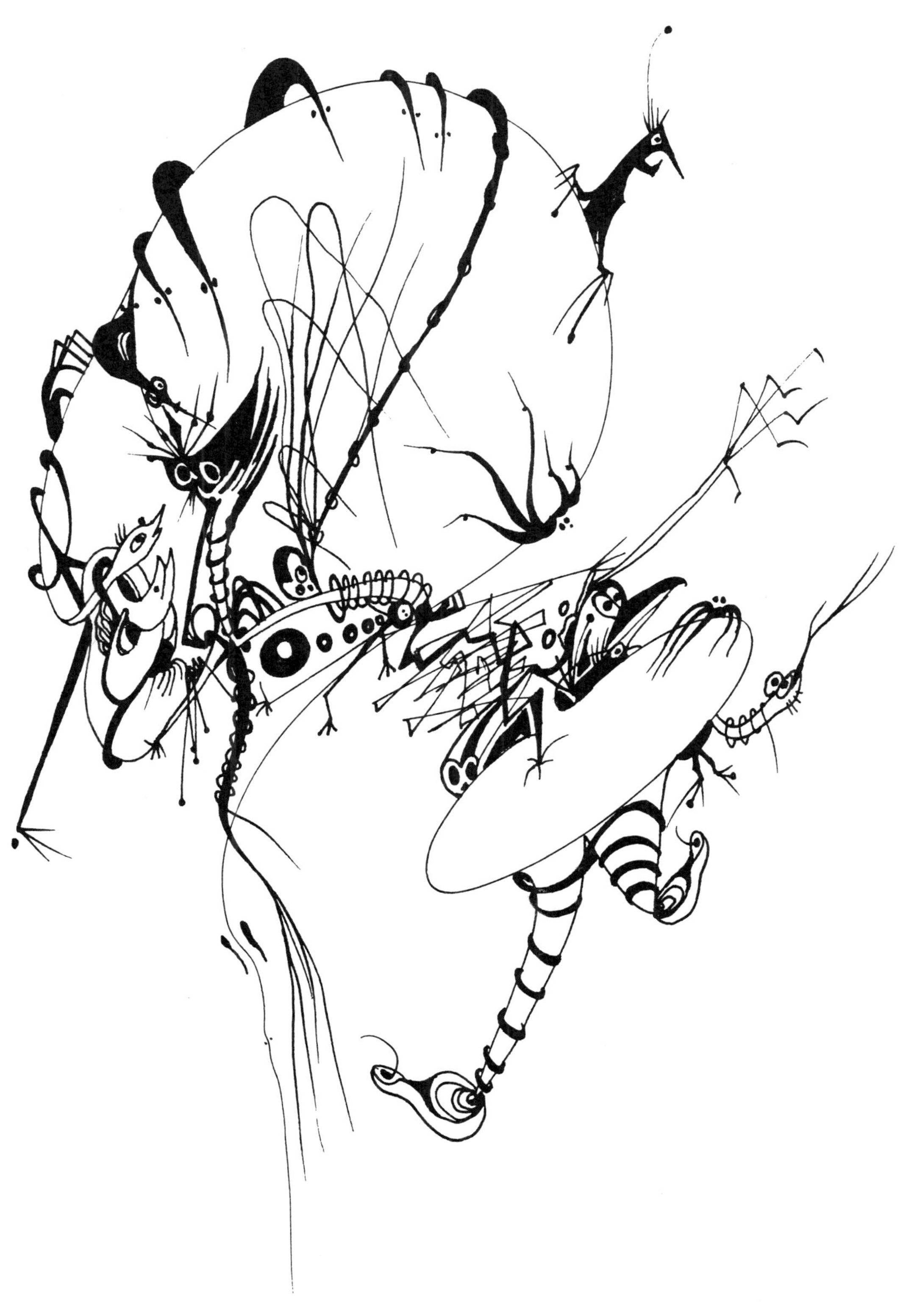

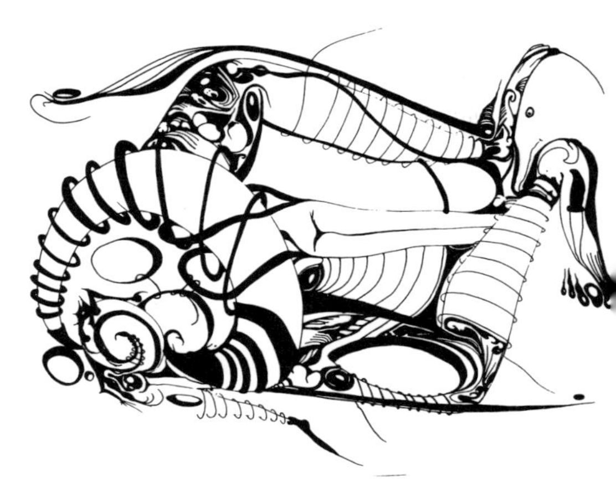

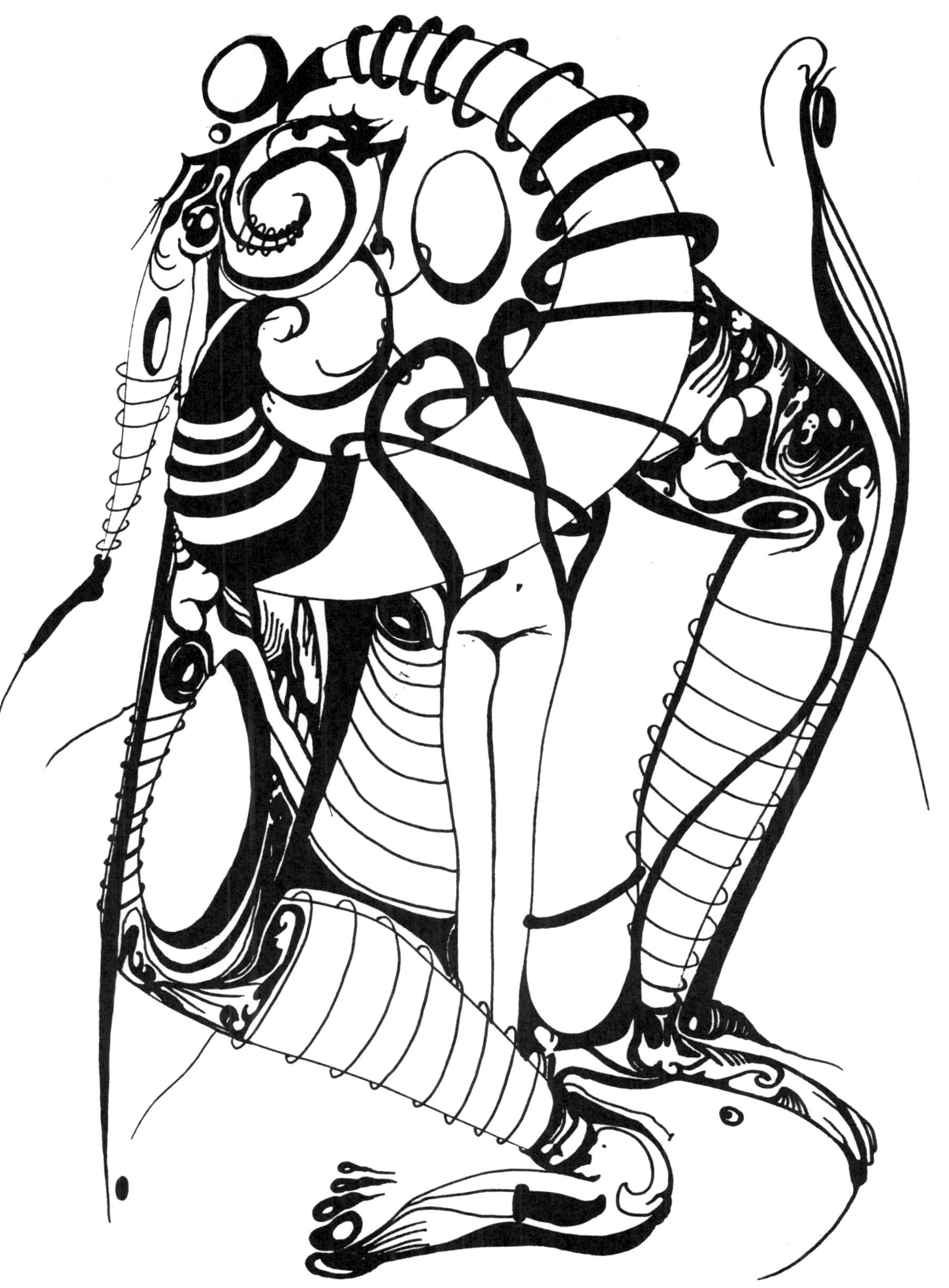

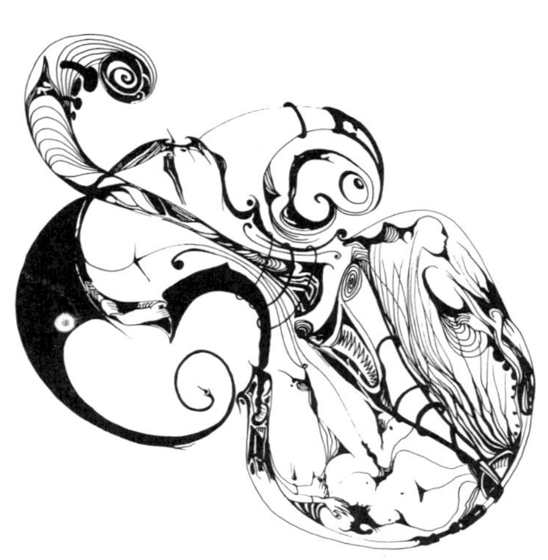

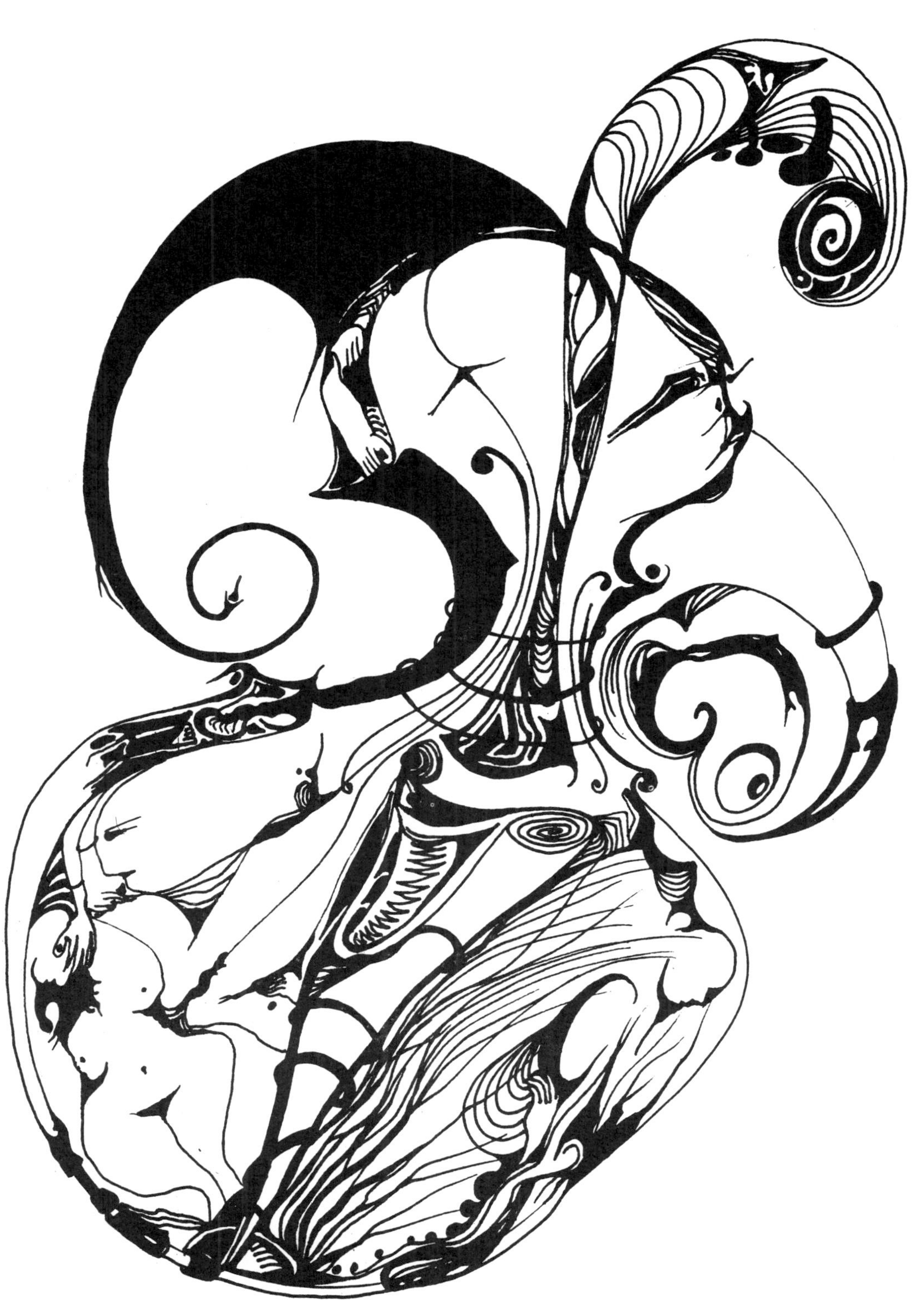

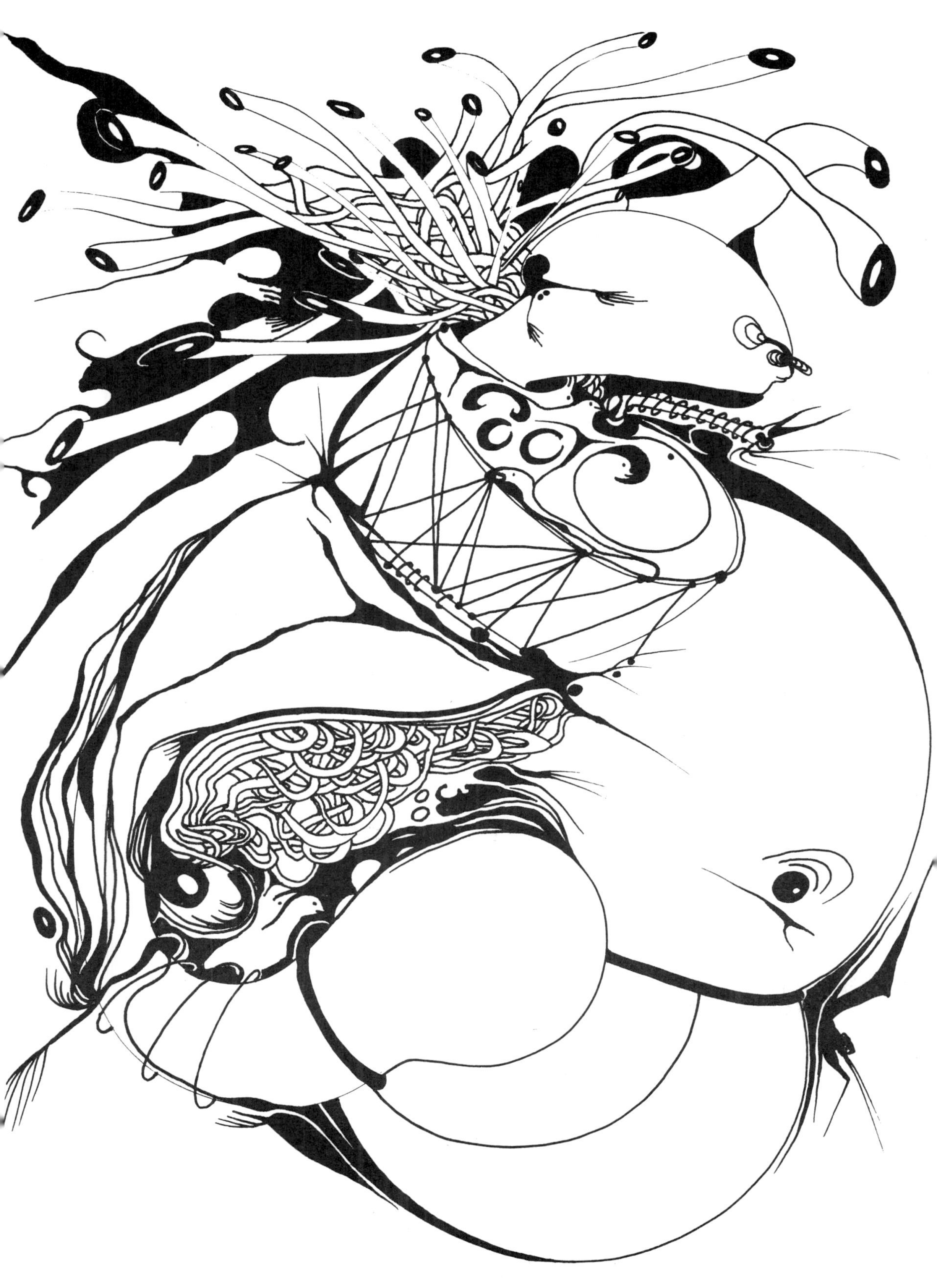

GRAND FINALE

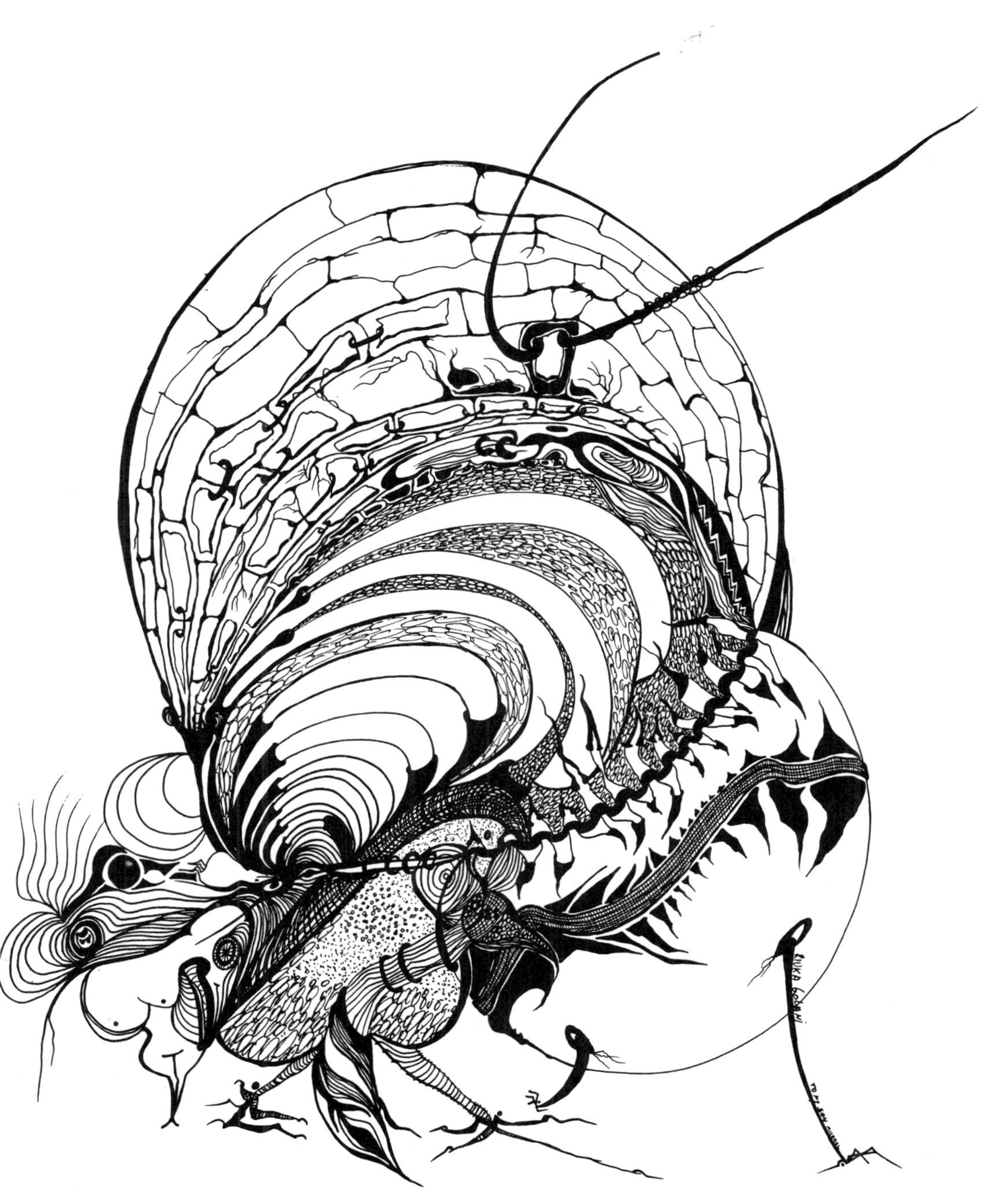

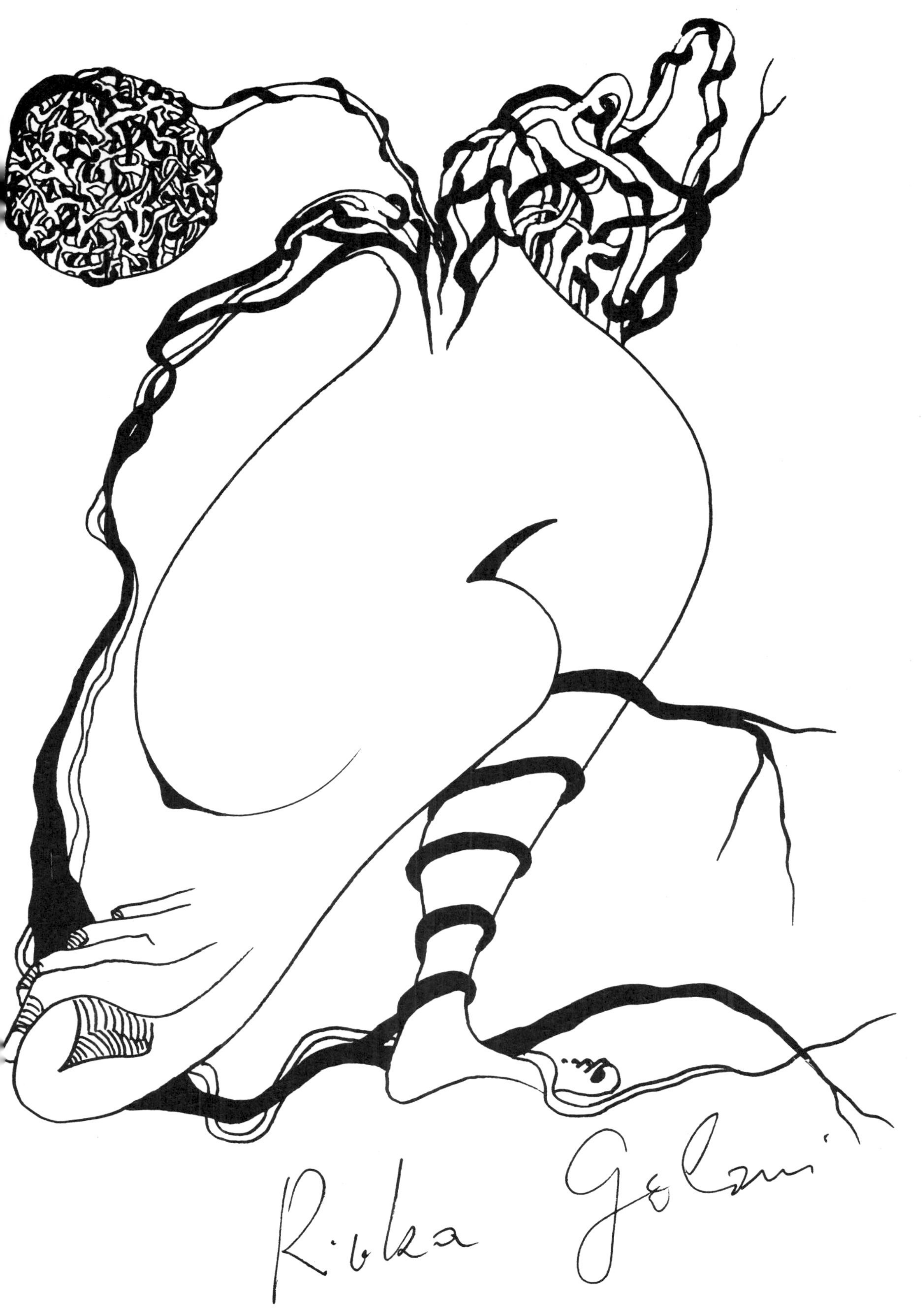
Rivka Golani